13 Weeks to *Joy*

Also by Jennifer Jill Schwirzer

13 Weeks to Love
13 Weeks to Peace
Damsel, Arise!

13 Weeks to Joy

How to Hold the Happiness God Gives

JENNIFER JILL SCHWIRZER

Pacific Press®
Publishing Association

Nampa, Idaho | www.pacificpress.com

Cover design by Steve Lanto
Cover design resources from iStockphoto.com | 108316241

Unless otherwise noted, Scripture quotations are from the New King James Version®. Copyright © 1982 by Thomas Nelson. Used by permission. All rights reserved.

Scripture quotations marked KJV are from the King James Version of the Bible.

Scripture quotations marked NASB are from the NEW AMERICAN STANDARD BIBLE®, copyright © 1960, 1962, 1963, 1968, 1971, 1972, 1973, 1975, 1977, 1995 by the Lockman Foundation. Used by permission. www .lockman.org.

Scripture quotations marked NIV are from THE HOLY BIBLE, NEW INTERNATIONAL VERSION®. Copyright © 1973, 1978, 1984, 2011 by Biblica, Inc.® Used by permission. All rights reserved worldwide.

The author assumes full responsibility for the accuracy of all facts and quotations as cited in this book.

Additional copies of this book may be purchased by calling toll-free 1-800-765-6955 or by visiting AdventistBookCenter.com.

Library of Congress Cataloging-in-Publication Data

Names: Schwirzer, Jennifer Jill, 1957- author.
Title: 13 weeks to joy : how to hold the happiness God gives / Jennifer Jill Schwirzer.
Description: Nampa : Pacific Press Publishing Association, 2019. | Summary: "A devotional about finding joy in Christ"— Provided by publisher.
Identifiers: LCCN 2019036731 | ISBN 9780816365746 (paperback) | ISBN 9780816365784 (kindle edition)
Subjects: LCSH: Spiritual life—Christianity. | Christian life.
Classification: LCC BV4501.3 .S3875 2019 | DDC 248.4/86732—dc23
LC record available at https://lccn.loc.gov/2019036731

September 2019

Contents

The "Odicy"

The "Odicy" is a play on words. *Theodicy* is a branch of religious study that explores the question of why a good God allows suffering. *The Odyssey* is a poem, written by the legendary Greek author Homer, about a returning king's journey to recover his queen and palace from interlopers. I like that the word *theodicy* sounds like *The Odyssey*. I also believe that theodicy is the real odyssey (no offense to Homer) because the best way to answer the question of theodicy—why God allows suffering—is to tell the odyssey of God's story, or what we call "the great controversy." The story of how God's character of love holds up under the titanic weight of earthly suffering is a wild one, even outstripping a Greek myth for drama and complexity. I propose we call it "the odicy."

So why address theodicy in a book about joy?

Because this book promotes a joyful response to life's hardships, we first need to establish a rational basis for such a response. I want to help us to be cheerful but not delusional. After all, if earthly existence with all of its suffering is the end of the story, positive thinking rings hollow. The reason we rejoice, the reason we reframe the trials of life and even thank God for them, is because reality really is, ultimately, positive. Apart from that fact, positivity looks crazy.

You suffer, have suffered, and will suffer. You know and love other suffering people. You picked up this book to find out how to find positive emotions in the midst of all the suffering. That shift is God's leading. You can't truly rejoice in suffering without supernatural help and divine logic. So the first step in learning joy is understanding God well enough to trust Him, and trusting Him enough to give Him access to your heart. To do this, you must ask why He allows suffering. You must have at least a basic understanding of "the odicy"—the epic story of how a good God came to allow the existence of evil and the suffering that flows from it.

Some people say we shouldn't ask God why. "We will never know," they sigh. "God is so mysterious." And while we may not understand the particulars of why God allowed Joe to live but Tim died when his car was T-boned by a drunk driver, we can understand the big-picture dynamics and principles involved. Besides, Jesus asked why. Traumatized and confused, He cried out on the cross, "Why have you forsaken Me?" Don't we also feel forsaken at times? Can't we cry out for answers? Can't God take it on the chin when we don't understand Him and just say so? The human mind reflexively seeks to make meaning out of life. Doesn't this God-given impulse imply the existence of meaning? Doesn't God provide believable, logical, satisfying answers to our aching questions? Why would God bestow upon us the gift of reason, then tell us not to use it? Doesn't God make sense? I think so, and because I do, the next few pages will be my attempt to share a sensible theodicy.

A sweeping overview

"The odicy" began with—and centers on—Jesus. "In the beginning was the Word, and the Word was with God, and the Word was God. He was in the beginning with God. All things were made through Him, and without Him nothing was made that was made" (John 1:1–3). The eternal, divine Jesus who made all things even made the angel Lucifer who ultimately betrayed Him. "All things have been created through him and for him" (Colossians 1:16, NIV). God created the angelic hosts with the power of choice. So long as they freely obeyed the law of unselfish love that governed the universe, the glories and joys of heaven would continue. But Lucifer perverted his God-given freedom into license. Lucifer, the "son of the morning" who stood in the direct, illustrious presence of God, basked in His approval and honor as a leader of the angels (Isaiah 14:12). When little by little he began to cherish a spirit of self-exaltation, God said of him: "Your heart became proud on account of your beauty" (Ezekiel 28:17, NIV). From there, Lucifer engaged in a revolt of epic proportions, rallying the angels against God and attempting to unseat Him from His throne.

We don't know how long God labored to turn him around, but Lucifer proved intractable. More than this, he had brainwashed a third of the angels (Revelation 12). God finally decided to cut His losses and go to war against His frenemy and his followers. Can you imagine? God loved Lucifer, but forced by circumstances to contain the damage of Lucifer's now toxic influence, the Creator mounted an attack on His created one. After the attack, a deep well of grief brewed in the heart of God as He pieced together His losses.

The most significant injuries sustained in heaven's war were the security and stability of the angelic hosts. The war had ended but not the war of emotions. Heaven was still in psychological tumult. The angels were bonded to Lucifer, but they loved God too. Like children of divorcing parents, they longed for harmony between the authority figures of their heavenly home. In earthly courts of justice, we disqualify relatives from serving on a jury for another relative's trial on the basis of emotional bias created by a familial bond. The angels held that bias toward both God and Lucifer, and it tore them in two. While externally loyal to God, they remained internally conflicted. God dealt tenderly with this conflict, as He deals tenderly with ours. Out of His infinite patience and justice, and with creative genius, He approached the task of revealing the truth about the nefarious character of Lucifer-turned-Satan by shedding the dazzling light of divine love in yet brighter beams. In order to do this, He would create an order of being so much like Him that He could say, "Look at them, and you will see Me." That's us, humans. We're God's masterpiece, and in a sense, His weapon.

"So God created mankind in his own image; in the image of God he created them; male and female he created them" (Genesis 1:27, NIV). *Image* means "reproduction" or "representation," alluding to God's desire for us to unveil His heart of steadfast love to "the principalities and powers in the heavenly places"—those emotionally scarred angels who had stood with God in the conflict (Ephesians 3:10). After all, even in the human realm, the accused need witnesses to speak on their behalf. In supreme humility, God said, "You are My witnesses" (Isaiah 43:12) and placed us on the stage of planet Earth as "a spectacle to the world, both to angels and to men" (1 Corinthians 4:9).

Because love and freedom are inextricably entwined, because true love is a choice, all of God's created beings possess a functional, self-directed free will. Knowing that free will can turn very, very bad and that Lucifer, now Satan, lurked on planet Earth to tempt us, God did what any responsible parent does: He created a contingency plan to provide for His kids in the event of a disaster. He vowed,

"Though the mountains be shaken
   and the hills be removed,
yet my unfailing love for you will not be shaken
   nor my covenant of peace be removed" (Isaiah 54:10, NIV).

God's "covenant of peace" is His eternal pledge to save us at any cost to Himself. When humanity fell into sin, God mobilized the covenant of peace by promising and then sending His own dear Son to join the human race. Jesus would become "the last Adam," filling the office that Adam had left vacant (1 Corinthians 15:45). Jesus' perfect life and atoning death would represent humanity before God to such an extent that God could save any who embraced them by faith. Because "the gifts and the calling of God are irrevocable," the purpose of God to use humanity to reveal His self-giving love would still stand (Romans 11:29).

God's method

What jumps out from this story so far is God's method of dealing with evil. Rather than swoop in like a cartoon superhero to vanquish it, He takes the long but more thorough route; He inoculates His creation against sin by giving evil some space to reveal its true character. This method, though slower, more agonizing, and more tedious, accomplishes what a shock-and-awe, fire-and-brimstone decimation of God's enemy fails to accomplish. It allows for sin's true character to manifest itself. Ultimately, in allowing for the demonstration of the character of sin, God is being truthful.

He is also being effective. John Peckham says, "No amount of power exercised by a king would prove to his subjects that he is not unjust. No show of executive power could clear the name of a president accused of corruption. A conflict over character cannot be settled by sheer power but requires demonstration."[1]

This slow-but-thorough approach is doubly necessary because, with our fallen natures, we possess an inherent blindness to the true nature of sin. The only way God can fortify us internally against the sin that would defile heaven all over again is to allow its ghastly heart to be revealed. In order for that exposure to take place, sin needs a platform. God must allow Satan space and opportunity to act out the dictates of his malevolent soul.

God presides over the universe in awesome, life-giving majesty, yet even a cursory look at His creation shows a will other than God's exerting itself continually in the death spirals of disease, natural disaster, and man's inhumanity to man. While God does reign, He allows the enemy's work more freedom than we would like. But the freedom God grants to Satan coalesces with the divine purpose ultimately to place the universe on the solid ground of certainty about God's love and Satan's evil.

In considering "the odicy," we must maintain a careful symmetry that blends divine sovereignty and human free will. If we emphasize sovereignty and minimize free will, we will conclude that the only will active in suffering is God's. Everything becomes God's will—no ifs, ands, buts, or qualifiers—making it seem as though God desires sin and suffering. Well-meaning Christians make this mistake often. "Well, it must have been God's will," we say to a mother at her child's graveside. Wait! That child was walking to school, and a drunk driver ran her down. Satan tempted the driver to drink at eight in the morning, and the driver succumbed. God may not have intervened, but the horrifying nature of the child's death reveals the devil's will and heart, not God's.

If, on the other hand, we emphasize free will and minimize sovereignty, we make it seem that God lacks power. I once counseled a couple who had been told by a pastor after their baby died that, essentially, the devil did it and God stood by watching, unable to stop him. In striving to avoid presenting the tragedy as God's fault, the pastor hoped to comfort the parents by avoiding one imbalance, but he succumbed to another. As the parents considered the prospect of a universe in which the devil has unlimited free reign, they became even more distressed. God sees the sparrow fall. He "sits enthroned over the flood" (Psalm 29:10, NIV). He "works all things according to the counsel of His will" (Ephesians 1:11). It may be difficult for our finite minds to comprehend how this can be, but the limits of our human reasoning don't alter the reality that God is both freedom granting and sovereign.

Innocent suffering

God allows the enemy space to create his chaos, but the sin and the suffering that convulse our aching planet don't reflect the perfect will and heart of God any more than a messy child's room reflects the will of a tidy parent. Why, then, does God overrule in some cases but not all? He certainly possesses the power to overrule, and He does at times. He opened the Red Sea and the Jordan River, raised people from the dead, gave sight to the blind, and healed all manner of diseases. To someone longing for a similar miracle, such stories can seem like cruel taunts. It's easy to take it personally when God lets the devil have his way with us. This is especially true when we have done nothing to deserve this pain. The troubles we bring on ourselves don't pose the problem, but the *innocent* suffering that assaults our sense of justice. Can't God at least match the suffering with the sin? Can't He transfer the four-year-old's brain tumor to the skull of a terrorist? Can't He drive the hurricane out of the path of a poor man's hut and toward a rich man's vacation home? Can't He make things fair?

In terms of power, yes, He can; however, in terms of character, He can't. For God to confine sin within boundaries of justice would be to mask its true character. Sin is lawlessness. Sin is the reason a sweet, young girl bringing bread to her grandmother loses a leg to a land mine in Afghanistan. Sin is the reason a loving mother at church who ran the food pantry dies of cancer at forty years old. Sin is the reason innocent puppies die in puppy mills, and all "creation groans" (Romans 8:22). In order to reveal the heart of good and evil, God must allow sin to show its true, death-saturated colors.

In Jesus' parable of the wheat and the tares in Matthew 13:24–30, the farmer told the servants not to try to pull up the newly sprouted tares, lest the newly sprouted wheat be uprooted as well. He flatly admitted that "an enemy has done this," yet he enjoined a postponement of the enemy's eradication (verse 28). In the same way, God postpones His final dealings with evil because He will more successfully eradicate it in the end if He allows it to flourish temporarily. We are cautioned not to pass judgment "before the time" (1 Corinthians 4:5). Uprooting sin and its consequences now would lead to preventable, collateral damage and would fall short of accomplishing God's ultimate agenda of demonstrating the truth.

Here is the dilemma of "the odicy," as written by C. S. Lewis: "If God were good, He would wish to make His creatures perfectly happy, and if God were almighty He would be able to do what He wished. But the creatures are not happy. Therefore God lacks either goodness, or power, or both."[2]

But there is a third option. Option three is that God is good and wants to end suffering; He is almighty and able to end suffering, but He is also love and has chosen, for a greater purpose, not to unilaterally end suffering until His mission is completed. That greater purpose is to reveal His unspeakable love and, in that glorious context, to unveil the true nature of sin, thus inoculating human beings against it for eternity.

Like the cancer patient opting to lose her hair to chemotherapy in order to destroy a tumor, or a doctor amputating a gangrenous limb, God can't solve the big-picture problem of sin without allowing some smaller-picture damage to occur. We may humbly trust Him, knowing that "God's children must meet trials and difficulties. But they should accept their lot with a cheerful spirit, remembering that for all that the world neglects to bestow, God Himself will make up to them in the best of favors."[3]

Dominions

Like any war, the great controversy entails rules of engagement that God, as a supremely moral Being, respects. We learn something of these rules when we examine the concept of dominions.

God had created the sinless Adam to "have dominion" over the earth, but through partaking of the forbidden fruit, he forfeited his dominion into the hands of Satan (Genesis 1:26; Psalm 8:6). The devil made this transfer clear when he later offered dominion back to Jesus, saying, "All this authority I will give You, and their glory; *for this has been delivered to me*, and I give it to whomever I wish" (Luke 4:6; emphasis added). Tragically, he has become "the ruler of this world" (John 12:31; 14:30; 16:11), "the god of this age" (2 Corinthians 4:4), and "the prince of the power of the air, the spirit who now works in the sons of disobedience" (Ephesians 2:2). In other words, Adam forfeited the governance of planet Earth to Satan when he chose to partake of the forbidden fruit.

Something similar to supernatural dominions play out in earthly international affairs. The drug lord Juan Matta-Ballesteros had done his share of damage in trafficking drugs into the United States. Fed up with his various crimes, Honduran law enforcement agents and US Marshals raided his home in Tegucigalpa, Honduras, and sent in a team to cart him off for trial and incarceration. Ballesteros is still in the United States, serving three life sentences. After his arrest, Honduran protestors took to the streets, enraged that US Marshals came upon their soil to arrest and extradite a citizen, thus breaking the country's constitution. Five people died in the melee. In the eyes of the protesters, the United States violated Honduran dominion by arresting and extraditing Matta-Ballesteros on Honduran soil.

In spite of Satan's havoc-wreaking activities, God invades Satan's dominion when we ask for His aid and when He knows it would be for the best. According to Daniel's vision, the Son of man, who created dominions, allows the beasts to have dominion for a time (see Daniel 7; Colossians 1:16). However, the Son of man ultimately receives this dominion back forever (Daniel 7:14). Through Jesus, the grand narrative will come to completion. Jesus in the capacity of our self-sacrificing, self-humbling, incarnate God will win dominion back and return it to us as He makes us "kings and priests" (Revelation 1:6; 5:10; see also Revelation 20:6). Jesus delegated dominion to us in Eden; He will return it to us in Eden restored, the new earth.

How will Jesus ultimately win the battle? This supernatural war rolls out on the battlefield of the psyche. The win goes to the one who obtains the loving allegiance of human beings. The battle is won not by power alone but by the power of love. The turf war is over the heads and hearts of God's creatures. God must persuade us by allowing the enemy to have dominion for a time and by showing that He is love and that sin is not love.

This dominion won't be regained through military might or prowess but through winning heart-level citizen loyalty. Jesus won the right to restored dominion on the cross, but to transfer that right back to us requires our consent, both collectively and individually. The legal arrangements for our reinstatement have been made, but our personal acceptance of the agreement ratifies the process. God has spent six millennia persuading human beings that He is worthy of their worship and obedience. Those who respond have a "right to the tree of life" (Revelation 22:14, NIV). Finally, a new humanity in Christ will take up residence in the new earth, Eden restored.

Talk about second chances!

In granting Satan dominion, God merely respects the very free will with which He created us. He respected and honored the free will of Adam as he relinquished the dominion of our fair planet to the hands of His enemy. Then He respected the free will of Satan as he turned our fair planet into a place of chaos and suffering. He respects the free will of each inhabitant of planet Earth as they make their choices, moment by moment, whether to yield to the invitation of His Spirit or the temptations of the devil. While God grants freedom, He uses the effects of that freedom for His own purposes, ultimately winning back dominion heart by heart until

"The kingdom and dominion,
And the greatness of the kingdoms under the whole heaven,

Shall be given to the people, the saints of the Most High. . . .
And all dominions shall serve and obey Him" (Daniel 7:27).

God wins "the odicy" by allowing the truth about Himself and His enemy to be revealed in crystal clarity. This can't be done while stifling, micromanaging, and harnessing Satan. God must let him play out his dark motives until they effectively dull the gloss of his pretty lies.

God doesn't just tell; He shows. He demonstrated "His own love toward us" at the cross when Satan's thirst for blood overwhelmed his attempts to hide his true motives (Romans 5:8). Caught up in the frenzy of crucifying Jesus, wholly intoxicated by his pure hatred of God, the devil exposed himself for who he really was. Against that black backdrop, the light of God's love revealed itself in brilliant distinction.

God gave His dear Son to win back the human family. He made the ultimate sacrifice. The Cross is the ultimate statement and the unmistakable proof that God would withhold nothing good from us. "He who did not spare His own Son, but delivered Him up for us all, how shall He not with Him also freely give us all things?" (Romans 8:32). If Jesus would sacrifice His union with the Father, even pour out life itself, would He withhold anything? If I would give you the keys to my house, would I withhold my thrift-store furniture? God proved His utter generosity when He gave Himself. Life on the earth is a muddy window through which we see some of God and some of His enemy, but the Cross is an open door. It leaves no doubt or confusion as to the heart of God. When we look to the events of life on earth for consistent, reliable information about God, we look to the wrong source for evidence. When we look to the Cross, we find a clear path forward.

Choosing joy

Many others have done a better job than I ever could of explaining theodicy. I will work within the scope of my expertise. Most of our arguments against God are emotional. We are disappointed that He didn't come through for us, protect us, or bless us in the way we had hoped. Let me address those disappointments. First, He can take it—He understands that this great-controversy stuff is difficult. But of more importance is the fact that He joins us. Remember, even Jesus asked why. Jesus also experienced disappointment with God. Our God understands our issues with God. To balance that out, we have a choice. We can cherish faith, or we can nurse our doubts. I am hoping and praying that this book will encourage the former.

Stanford professor T. M. Luhrmann has observed church life as an anthropologist. She has concluded that when people see God as good, it makes them healthier: "I saw that people were able to learn to experience God in this way, and that those who were able to experience a loving God vividly were healthier—at least, as judged by a standardized psychiatric scale." She also said, "When God was experienced as remote or not loving, the more someone prayed, the more psychiatric distress she seemed to have; when God was experienced as close and intimate, the more someone prayed, the less ill he was."[4] Apparently, it's not religion itself that brings us benefits but our picture of God and our choices as they relate to that view that heal us.

Although God won't make us perfectly happy here on earth now, He does promise the gift of joy in the midst of our sorrows. May we all find that joy is my prayer.

DISCUSSION QUESTIONS

1. What events in your life have led you to question God?

2. If you had just a few sentences to explain why God allows sin and suffering, what would you say?

3. How do you imagine God feels as He allows temporary suffering for the greater purpose of eradicating sin?

4. How do you imagine the loyal angels felt when the conflict arose between Lucifer and God?

5. How does God's method of eradicating evil differ from the typical human methods?

6. Why is it important to maintain a balance between an emphasis of God's sovereignty and human free will?

7. What are some instances of innocent suffering that have led you to feel the utter unfairness of sin?

8. God can end all innocent suffering in terms of power. But how does His character prevent Him from ending it?

9. How can an unloving, distant view of God actually make religion into a vehicle for more distress?

10. Have you had any ah ha moments about the character of God? Describe them.

---

1. John C. Peckham, *Theodicy of Love: Cosmic Conflict and the Problem of Evil* (Grand Rapids, MI: Baker Academic, 2018), 91.

2. C. S. Lewis, *The Problem of Pain* (New York: HarperOne, 2009), 16.

3. Ellen G. White, *The Ministry of Healing* (Mountain View, CA: Pacific Press®, 1905), 199.

4. T. M. Luhrmann, "The Benefits of Church," *New York Times*, Opinion, April 20, 2013, https://www.nytimes.com/2013/04/21/opinion/sunday/luhrmann-why-going-to-church-is-good-for-you.html.

Dealings With Feelings

From the time Sue Johnson was six years old, an intense curiosity about relationships brewed in her mind. Night after night, she sat on the dark stairs of her home in Chatham, England, and listened as the two people she loved most in the world—her parents—emotionally ripped each other apart. "I moved from being anguished to mesmerized," she says. "What was this desperate drama all about?"

Sue's family owned a pub, which gave her many more opportunities to observe human relationships. Conceptualizing interpersonal emotional patterns as dances, she says, "There were moments when the emotional music and the steps of the dancers shifted dramatically in tone and color. But I didn't know what it meant."

Eventually, Sue learned what these moments meant. A grown-up Sue emigrated to Canada and decided to become a psychologist. "One day, I walked into my first couple's therapy session. And there, waiting for me, was the same mesmerizing drama I remembered. Only this time, I was supposed to be able to help people out of it!"[1]

Sue Johnson got her "aha moment" sometime later after listening to a lecture about couple's therapy that dismissed the importance of emotions and bonding. Most therapists at the time didn't really believe in adult bonding, and this frustrated Sue. The prevailing sentiment in the field of counseling eschewed so-called enmeshment so strongly that it almost seemed to discard the idea of attachment entirely. Inspired to learn the steps of the dance of emotions in relationships, Sue worked with a team to develop *emotionally focused therapy* (EFT). Not surprisingly, emotionally focused therapy centers on emotion. "It's an attachment approach, so it assumes that we all have very deep needs for safe connection and emotional contact, and that when we don't get those needs [met], we get stuck in very negative interactional patterns; the dance music gets very complicated."[2]

Those negative interactional patterns abound in the human experience, don't they? Take one isolated issue: criticism. While some criticism is necessary, the general human trend is to be overly critical. A recent study of sixty business leadership teams showed that the ideal positive-to-negative feedback ratio hovers around five to one; a similar ratio has been shown to work best in marriage.[3] The sad fact is that the *real* ratio is reversed: we give far more negative feedback than positive in our relationships, particularly close relationships. On the one hand, this is understandable. On an emotional level, close relationships can resemble two people stuffed into a closet. We need to ask for changes from the other to make ourselves comfortable, but we overdo it.

For an exercise that can help married couples and others communicate their emotions effectively, check out "Communicating Emotions" in the toolbox.

Human beings default to the negative, so healthy positivity in relationships comes through intentional, conscious efforts rather than luck. Social scientists have demonstrated that the brain reacts more strongly to negative stimuli, which brings about a greater surge in electrical activity.[4] Negative information sticks in the brain more easily than positive information, leading us to weigh the negative more heavily than we do the positive. This is why many countries have laws preventing media coverage and certain public discussions while issues are *sub judice* ("under judicial consideration"). It's not that we would *admit* to believing the tabloids; it's that we would be *influenced* by them subconsciously because the messages stick.

We are a race of pessimists. The human heart tends to default toward negative feelings, such as sadness, anxiety, anger, and disappointment. Substances become an easy way to numb these negative emotions: nearly 5 percent of the world's population suffers from alcoholism; over 22 percent use nicotine habitually; and more than 3 percent use cannabis.[5] There is an opioid crisis in the United States: "More than 11 million people abused prescription opioids in 2016."[6]

Fortunately, the story doesn't end there. While our emotional natures may be bent toward negativity, they were originally shaped by the Creator to hold extremely positive emotions. Living in the shadows violates our design and causes us harm, especially as the negativity accumulates over the years. Much of growing in Jesus—more than we have realized, I think—amounts to allowing God's Holy Spirit to loosen our grip on the dark daggers of fear, pain, guilt, shame, and anger and to help us instead seize trust, pleasure, peace, confidence, forgiveness, love, and joy.

We can wake up with a cheerful, "Good morning, God," or a scowling, "Good God, it's morning," on our lips. We can fulfill our capacity for positive emotions, or we can lapse into the negativity of our fallen natures. Dealing with our feelings means we expand toward the positive.

Secondary disturbance

Yet assuming that we should experience nothing but positive feelings is another extreme and will lead us to practice avoidance. If we avoid negative feelings at all costs, we may develop *secondary disturbance*, which is to get upset about being upset. Examples include feeling guilty about being angry at someone, anxiety about being embarrassed, or depressed about having panic attacks.

Often people become more disturbed about being disturbed than they were disturbed in the first place. That is silly because it's OK to be disturbed, which means it's OK to be disturbed about being disturbed, too; however, the point is that we ultimately want to resolve the disturbance, even though it's OK!

Secondary disturbance comes in two basic forms: pathologizing and moralizing. When we pathologize disturbance, we overestimate the harm it will do to us physically and psychologically. Pathologized negative emotions express themselves in statements such as, "I'm going to have a heart attack!" "I'll just die!" "This is going to kill me." Moralizing our disturbance sees it as constituting a failure, as in the following expressions: "I'm a Christian; I'm not supposed to be sad!" "My fear means I have no faith!" "I shouldn't feel this way."

How do we resolve secondary disturbance? First, accept those negative emotions, as contradictory as that may seem. In healthy emotionality, we maintain a careful tension between two things: accepting negative emotions, and counterintuitively but still correctly, seeking to resolve them. When facing emotional distress, we tend to veer into an either-or mode, when the healthiest route is actually both-and. We needn't choose *either* accepting our negative feelings *or* trying to improve them; we may embrace them and, at the same time, welcome the process of returning to positivity.

What makes us emotionally unhealthy is not the *presence* of negative emotions but the *process* of negative emotions. How do we handle those distressing brain signals? With acceptance and intentionality, or by catastrophizing, stuffing, or a myriad of other un-healthy patterns?

Happiness

As the United States Declaration of Independence says, the Creator endowed us with certain unalienable rights—life, liberty, and the pursuit of happiness. Happiness can be a slippery little fish, though, because it tends to come best as the by-product of a higher pursuit than personal pleasure. Because God created us for self-giving love, and we thrive best in service to others, the motivation to make ourselves happy can militate against our best—and happiest—selves. However, pursuing happiness as a feature of good stewardship is a different story. If God created us with the capacity for joy, can't we unselfishly strive to reach our potential for His glory and for the benefit of His other children? By stewarding our emotions in the same way we care for our bodies, we can pursue happiness from an altruistic motive.

The pursuit of happiness must be engineered carefully to coalesce with life on a broken planet. We will, at times, face unutterable grief, disappointment, loss, and suffering. If we are to live authentically, we must allow for the stretching of our hearts into uncomfortable shapes. Stuffing, denying, or numbing away negative emotions will prevent the deepening of our souls. God designed us to reflect His character, and lives lived rightly are in the constant process of becoming more and more like Him. Because "thoughts and feelings combined make up the moral character,"[7] and God calls us to be "transformed into his image," becoming more and more like Him in character, we can fully expect that with each growth spurt we will think and feel more the way God thinks and feels (2 Corinthians 3:18, NIV).

God's emotions

How does God experience emotion? Profoundly. That massive heart—the beat of which sends the life pulse through the universe—holds more emotion than we will ever know. First and foremost, God loves. Yes, I know that divine love isn't just a feeling. But the most principled love forms the basis for the most powerful affection. The most intensely positive emotions of love flow out of the kind of steadfast love that perseveres in spite of negative emotions. God doesn't allow His feelings to control Him, but He feels and feels very deeply. The affection He feels for His children spills out in thousands of sacred messages found in His Word.

God's love forms the seedbed of every other divine emotion; none of His feelings contradict His baseline state of absolute others-centeredness. For example, God's compassion flows out of His love:

As a father pities his children,
So the LORD pities those who fear Him.
For He knows our frame;
He remembers that we are dust (Psalm 103:13, 14).

Sometimes God's feelings seem incongruous with love, such as when He regretted that He had made humankind (Genesis 6:6, 7). Could it be that in such passages God expresses deep *emotions* of regret while He remains firm in His steadfast love? Could it be that in such cases God is being authentic about what goes on in His heart? God certainly experiences grief on a level deeper than our smaller hearts can. Listen to Him grieve over the rebellions of His people:

"How can I give you up, Ephraim?
How can I hand you over, Israel?
How can I make you like Admah?
How can I set you like Zeboiim?
My heart churns within Me;
My sympathy is stirred" (Hosea 11:8).

Some people push back against the idea of God experiencing anger, but if we believe the Bible, it couldn't be clearer. It mentions God's wrath hundreds of times, often using a word that means "to snort," indicating its visceral nature. God's kind of anger is different from ours: His springs from love, but ours is from self-love. Yet God's ire is similar enough to human ire to share such labels as "wrath," "anger," and "indignation." God feels righteous indignation when the powerful exploit the weak, and so do we! God also experiences disgust, as shown in the following statement: "Because you are lukewarm, and neither cold nor hot, I will vomit you out of My mouth" (Revelation 3:16).

Basic emotions

Various models of human emotion abound. Some people say there are seven basic emotions, others eight, and still others ten. The most recent research says there are four core emotions: "happy, sad, afraid/surprised, and angry/disgusted."[8]

	Primary emotion	Secondary emotions	Tertiary emotions
Pre-Fall	Love	Affection, attraction, longing	Adoration, fondness, liking, lust, tenderness
	Joy	Cheer, optimism, energy	Bliss, delight, elation, triumph, excitement
	Peace	Tranquility, satisfaction, relief	Repose, calmness, contentment, gratitude, comfort
	Awe	Surprise, shock, wonder	Astonishment, stun, startle, admiration, fascination
Post-Fall	Sadness	Disappointment, hurt, loneliness	Hopelessness, gloom, grief, misery, dejection
	Shame	Guilt, remorse, regret	Condemnation, self-loathing, rejection, embarrassment, humiliation
	Fear	Horror, nervousness, worry	Apprehension, distress, dread, panic, alarm
	Anger	Irritation, rage, disgust	Exasperation, frustration, hate, jealousy, loathing

This wonderful spectrum of emotion fans out infinitely in secondary and tertiary forms and layer upon layer of affective complexity. These emotions can be felt simultaneously. Even as finite beings, we experience concurrent emotions when, for instance, an abusive relative goes to jail, yielding both relief and sadness, or when the exhilaration of falling in love interweaves with the fear of rejection.

For a worksheet to help you empathize with God's emotions, see "Connecting to God's Heart" in the toolbox.

How much more than we finite beings can God hold in His giant heart? God's wrath burns hot when His innocent children suffer abuse, but those perpetrating the abuse happen to be His beloved children too! What a mix of sadness and anger God must feel while watching this planet convulse in crime, war, and poverty. What adoration and joy must mingle with grief when one of His martyrs yields to the flames or the gallows, knowing the next thing this person will see is His face.

Admitting feelings

One of the most important steps we can take toward emotional maturity is to learn to identify and admit our own emotions. Coincidingly, one of the most important sentences we can learn is "I feel [fill in the blank]." Many of us have received flawed training when it comes to this skill. So many families never talk about their emotions. It's not that the emotions don't come out: they literally burst out in aggression; simmer via passive aggression; or smolder in depression, anxiety, or a myriad of other internalizations. Few individuals can identify their own emotions, and very few families frankly admit their true emotions to one another. This wrong training seems like a convenient way to do things, but it costs much more in the long run.

There's something about articulating our feelings that makes them manageable. I encourage those I help to expand their emotional vocabularies. While some fall into the trap of too closely studying their emotions, many lean toward the opposite pattern of failing to "become acquainted with the complicated moral machinery of the human heart."[9]

For a worksheet to help you identify your feelings, see "Feeling Tree" in the toolbox.

God asked the fallen Adam, "Where are you?" (Genesis 3:9). He asked the cowering Elijah, "What are you doing here, Elijah?" (1 Kings 19:13). He plies us with questions today through the Holy Spirit, leading us to examine our hearts to "see if there be any hurtful way" in us (Psalm 139:24, NASB). God leads us to introspection, and often, the first thing we encounter on the road to self-awareness is a big, fat feeling or two. The way we interact with those feelings determines whether we progress on the road to self-knowledge or stay stuck.

Most of our hard emotions begin with a desire to avoid soft emotions. The basic soft emotions include fear, sadness, pain, shame, and frustration. In order to cope with these highly vulnerable states, we callus them over with various forms of anger, annoyance, or coldness. As we express those hard emotions, we deepen their hold on us and drive the soft emotions down below, further into our subconscious. This is one reason we should avoid an excessive expression of hard emotions; it can harden us to the deepest, softest parts of ourselves.

Sadness	• Disappointment • Hurt • Loneliness
Shame	• Guilt • Remorse • Regret
Fear	• Horror • Nervousness • Worry
Anger	• Irritation • Rage • Disgust

I once counseled an estranged married couple whom I will call Sam and Jill. Sam would sit and vent his anger at Jill, and Jill would sit and vent her anger at Sam. I knew that they had each experienced pain and insecurity and that if we could get to those soft emotions, our counseling sessions would be more productive. I knew better than to counsel them together, given their level of anger. Early in my counseling career, I had learned that couples can fight like cats and dogs right in the session, so with Sam and Jill, I waited for one of them to show some vulnerability. Believe it or not, it was Sam—a professional, intelligent man with a very direct, unemotional way of talking. I watched him melt down into a little boy as he admitted his profound hurt that his wife didn't love him as he had hoped. I knew we had turned a corner and that there was hope for reconciliation. Vulnerability can be quite contagious, and Jill did follow Sam's lead.[10]

To ourselves, to God, to others

I recommend admitting feelings in three ways: to ourselves, to God, and to trusted loved ones. I remember feeling very stressed on a particular day and sensing that I might have a meltdown while going about my duties. It occurred to me to simply label my emotion. I said to myself, "I'm very aggravated," and the moment I did so, I felt an immediate wave of relief come over me. The first step of emotional regulation is emotion recognition.

Admitting our feelings to God can bring a similar relief; the best prayers come from our rawest cores. Speaking for myself, I am not the type to approach private prayer in a formal way. I talk to God as I would talk to my best friend as I go about my day, just free-associating through my thoughts and feelings as if in an extended counseling session. In my view, the most beautiful prayers in the Bible are the most emotional prayers:

- "My eyes overflow with rivers of water for the destruction of the daughter of my people" (Lamentations 3:48).
- "I am poured out like water, and all My bones are out of joint" (Psalm 22:14).
- "The thing I greatly feared has come upon me, and what I dreaded has happened to me" (Job 3:25).
- "My God, My God, why have You forsaken Me?" (Matthew 27:46).

God already knows what we feel. We might as well tell Him and remove every barrier to knowing that He understands us. Prayer can easily atrophy into a ritual observance rather than a rich, living conduit of loving communication between our souls and God. One way I have broken out of that is to make it a point to tell God exactly how I feel.

Finally, it can be very helpful to admit our feelings to others. Of course, this must be done carefully lest it degenerate into gossip, but actually owning our emotional response to a person or situation gives us more self-control and autonomy and prevents unhealthy venting such as gossip. Imagine, for instance, you have an unnerving experience with a coworker who loves to showboat his accomplishments. He bragged on and on during a company meeting, taking up the time allotted for you to share your own progress. The boss beamed at the coworker, and you felt as small as a mouse. Your own feelings are a strange mix of healthy exasperation and neurotic insecurity that your own value won't be recognized. Sitting and praying in your office, you admit your feelings of insecurity to God when suddenly your coworker comes in. He says, "Hey, sorry I blathered on like that in the meeting. I get insecure and overshare sometimes." That's an open door to be honest about your own feelings.

You say, "I felt exasperated and a little insecure myself." This honest sharing actually opens up a conversation that helps your coworker to see your personhood more clearly so that he doesn't walk over you as easily in the future.

Sue Johnson has learned that this honest sharing of soft emotions bonds people and at the same time helps them to retain their individuality. She says, "The more you know how to turn to other people, the more you can trust other people, . . . the stronger you are as a person, the better you feel about yourself and the more able you are to take autonomous decisions."[11] Sue has made it her life's work to help people admit, accept, and work with their deepest feelings. This quest has led her into a gold mine of emotional richness. If we can learn to see our emotions as wonderful assets, we will be blessed too.

DISCUSSION QUESTIONS

1. What was the criticism-to-affirmation ratio in your home growing up?

2. What is the criticism-to-affirmation ratio in your home now?

3. What kind of secondary disturbance regarding emotions have you experienced? Provide an example.

4. How does it affect you emotionally to contemplate the intense emotionality of God?

5. What are some of the positive functions of negative emotions?

6. Think of examples of when you have experienced each of the eight primary emotions.

7. What hard emotions have you used to protect yourself? Explain.

8. Who are the safe people in your life to whom you can admit your most vulnerable feelings?

9. How would you like your prayer life to be, moving into the future?

10. Vulnerability can be very awkward in the moment, but what are some of the long-term benefits?

1. Sue Johnson, "What Inspired Me to Write *Love Sense*?" Dr. Sue Johnson, January 3, 2014, http://www.drsuejohnson.com/love/what-inspired-me-to-write-love-sense/.

2. Sue Johnson, "Sue Johnson on Emotionally Focused Therapy," interview by Victor Yalom, Psychotherapy.net, July 20, 2011, https://www.psychotherapy.net/interview/sue-johnson-interview.

3. Jack Zenger and Joseph Folkman, "The Ideal Praise-to-Criticism Ratio," *Harvard Business Review*, March 15, 2013, https://hbr.org/2013/03/the-ideal-praise-to-criticism; Hara Estroff Marano, "Our Brain's Negative Bias," *Psychology Today*, last updated June 9, 2016, https://www.psychologytoday.com/us/articles/200306/our-brains-negative-bias.

4. Marano, "Our Brain's Negative Bias."

5. Linda R. Gowing et al., "Global Statistics on Addictive Behaviours: 2014 Status Report," abstract, *Addiction* 110, no. 6 (June 2015), https://doi.org/10.1111/add.12899.

6. American Physical Therapy Association, "7 Staggering Statistics About America's Opioid Epidemic," Move Forward, September 6, 2018, https://www.moveforwardpt.com/Resources/Detail/7-staggering-statistics-about-america-s-opioid-epi.

7. Ellen G. White, *Testimonies for the Church*, vol. 5 (Oakland, CA: Pacific Press®, 1889), 310.

8. Julie Beck, "New Research Says There Are Only Four Emotions," Health, *Atlantic*, February 4, 2014, https://www.theatlantic.com/health/archive/2014/02/new-research-says-there-are-only-four-emotions/283560/.

9. Ellen G. White to G. I. Butler, June 6, 1875, Lt. 16, 1875, Ellen G. White Estate, Silver Spring, MD, https://m.egwwritings.org/en/book/3598.2000001#23.

10. In this book, I will share clinical experiences but leave out any identifying information. Some of the cases are a blend of one or more cases.

11. Johnson, "Sue Johnson on Emotionally Focused Therapy."

Such a Shame

The kind of sexual abuse six-year-old Gabriel experienced brought with it an extra dose of shame simply because he was seduced, as opposed to forced. The eight-year-old abuser, who had his own story of sexual abuse in the foster system, had learned young how to manipulate others. Gabriel carried his secret, with its nucleus of fear that he was gay, through childhood. To disprove those fears, Gabriel became sexually active at thirteen years old, beginning a pattern of sexual conquest that lasted far into adulthood. Charged up by the thrill of the chase, Gabriel would target female after female, then lose interest and cast the woman away as soon as he had achieved his goal, leaving behind many broken hearts.

At seventeen, Gabriel discovered an even headier rush—methamphetamine. Plunging headlong into addiction, he kept up his supply by dealing. At twenty-one, he found himself in court, charged with the conspiracy to manufacture meth; the judge warned that he would go to prison if he reoffended. The fear of incarceration kept him clean for ten years until his live-in girlfriend became pregnant. "I'm not ready to be a father!" Gabriel objected. He urged her to abort the baby, but she refused. The child triggered Gabriel's unprocessed memories of his childhood abuse, which he tried to quiet through drugs and alcohol. Fully relapsing, Gabriel spun out of control into more than a decade of addiction. As is the case with substance abuse, the part of the brain responsible for the conscience and compassion becomes deactivated, and the baser, more animal impulses take over.

Years later, a man with a similar past introduced Gabriel to a loving, forgiving Jesus. Gabriel began to attend a Christian support group called Celebrate Recovery and found the strength from God and his faith family to leave these substances behind. Three years into his recovery, Gabriel came to me to work through some distressing traumas that continued to cause reactions. As we talked, the memories tumbled out. It was as if every time his mental bucket emptied, another load of memories came out of nowhere. I told Gabriel to brace himself for what could be a tough season of facing his history, long shrouded in a cloud of mind-altering substances.

Since Celebrate Recovery urges participants to make amends where possible, Gabriel searched on social media and in newspapers to find those who were wounded by his actions. The sheer magnitude of his sin, the disgraceful choices flowing out of a deadened conscience, horrified him. Drugs had numbed his sense of shame, and now it was coming back to life, with nerves prickling and stinging. I told him to believe in Jesus and to let the process unfold. The overwhelming guilt and shame stood like a mountain range past which he would find freedom. There was no going around it. More than this, he didn't even want to avoid feeling the distressing emotions that were proportionate to the pain he had caused others. It would have made light of their suffering and cheapened his repentance.

The foundational emotion

The first negative emotion to tear through the nervous systems of Adam and Eve was shame. Before they justified themselves with fig-leaf garments, before they cowered in fear, before they blamed and hated one another, before their spirits sunk in despair, before they even had a nanosecond to think, they felt the sting of shame on their newly fallen souls. Since then a torrent of shame has coursed through the human race, unstoppable and cruel, splitting off in every direction.

The foundational nature of shame can't be underestimated. Joseph Burgo, the author of *Shame: Free Yourself, Find Joy, and Build True Self-Esteem*, believes that "coping with shame is a daily preoccupation, not shame in the big toxic sense, but in a kind of everyday way."[1] Another shame expert, Gershen Kaufman, said, "Shame is the most disturbing experience individuals ever have about themselves; no other emotion feels more deeply disturbing because in the moment of shame the self feels wounded from within."[2] As the mother lode of all other distresses of the soul, shame feeds our basic human pain and fear so fully that to resolve shame is to transform a person completely from the inside out.

Shame morphs into countless forms of human brokenness. Many of us find ourselves in addictive cycles powered by shame. We sin to escape pain, wake up with a sin hangover, feel the crush of shame, which is about as painful an emotion as one can find, so what do we do? We sin again to numb the pain of shame. Shame drives relationship dysfunction in both its aggressive, narcissistic form, which is characterized by compensatory pride, and its compliant, codependent form, which is characterized by low self-esteem. Shame keeps us from opening up to love because we feel unworthy. At the same time, it makes us overly dependent upon human approval to anesthetize away the pain of our self-disapproval; then, it makes us critical toward those who fail to deliver. Shame drives the blame of others. Shame is a feeling so painfully vulnerable that we numb it with various pain-killing devices or try to deflect it with anger. Every human dilemma can be traced back, tributary by tributary, to the source spring that began to flow when humanity began to sin. We were naked and "not ashamed," and then in a split second, we were so ashamed that we desperately grasped fig leaves to relieve this strange, new agony (Genesis 2:25).

Shame to self-righteousness response

We might just pity ourselves as victims, but like rabid dogs, victims can be dangerous. We poor little sin victims are also little devils! Since the Fall, our reflexive response to shame is self-justification—a phenomenon nearly as universal as shame itself. Sin created a worthiness vacuum into which come our persistent human attempts to fill it. Having collectively lost our sense of God's approval, we stave off our feelings of unworthiness by attempting to entitle ourselves through various devices.

Typically, we bounce back and forth between two extremes built on the same foundation of self-merit: entitlement mentality and unworthiness. The *entitlement mentality* ignores our fallen status and presumptuously says we *are* worthy because of what we are, what we can do, or what we have. Unworthiness—a typical feeling religious people experience—says we are *not* worthy but that we can become worthy if we try hard enough. Self-justification reacts to the threat of unworthiness with a vigorous pushback that takes as many forms as there are individual personalities.

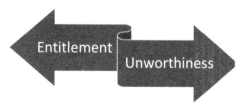

The human drive for worthiness has been explained scientifically in a phenomenon called the *licensing effect.* This unconscious reflex occurs when we do something that makes us feel virtuous and then use that to license a selfish deed. We will have a Diet Coke with a greasy cheeseburger, we will work an extra shift and then splurge on a luxury item we can't afford, or we will sacrifice for others and then spitefully demand recognition. Social scientists Anna Merritt, Daniel Effron, and Benoît Monin say of the licensing effect, "Past good deeds can liberate individuals to engage in behaviors that are immoral, unethical, or otherwise problematic."[3]

The licensing effect even affects social issues, such as matters of race. In one study, individuals who endorsed Barack Obama during the 2008 presidential election were more likely to express racist views in other contexts.[4] Some sociologists think that a nation that elected a black president subconsciously banked moral credit that, in turn, licensed voting for a president with white nationalist leanings.

But before you rush to social media to post against conservatives or liberals, let me share another source of the licensing effect: moral outrage. Research shows that expressing moral outrage is a tool we often use to alleviate our guilt over societal harm. One author of a recent study noted that Americans continued to buy Apple products ever after hearing reports of the dire working conditions at facilities in China where iPhones were manufactured. He says this failure to follow through on convictions stems from "the need to transfer the blame onto some other harm-doer, to find a bigger, badder bogeyman in order to vindicate ourselves."[5] Once vindicated through expressing our moral outrage, our consciences quiet down, and we can go back to living our hypocritical lives. Social media gives us a great opportunity to express moral outrage from the comfort of our own selfish lives.

Of course, the moral licensing effect works in reverse too. We often attempt to atone by following a deed that damages our sense of personal virtue with a good deed. Religious practices—from the indulgences of papal Rome during the Middle Ages to fasting and prayer as a means of self-purging—have been used to placate one's inner shame and replace moral credit since the beginning of time. This reversed moral licensing has mechanized religious hypocrisy for ages, explaining why the greatest vices can sometimes be found in the context of the most stringent religiosity. My work with victims of sexual abuse has opened my eyes to a dark world of licensing; for example, one man would pray with his daughter before raping her.

Our moral self-esteem can be robbed by others' shaming of us. I will illustrate this with my own frequent experience of trying to recover after being shamed by others. I have noticed that during the recovery period, my mind naturally drifts toward all the things I have done right—my virtues, my assets, and my righteousness. It is as if a huge withdrawal has been taken from my righteousness bank, and I feel driven to replace it. I am not unique—all of our shame-to-self-righteousness responses are predictable and reflexive. We will always try to replenish a shame-incurred deficit with righteousness of some kind.

Types of shame

The basic moral shame left by our sinful state tends to feather out into many other types of shame. Even those with no concept of sin, righteousness, holiness, or God suffer the effects of fallen Eden's core of shame, though they may not know what to call it. I believe that each of us carries a holding tank of moral shame that overflows into other kinds of shame. If we can somehow drain the tank, we will eliminate the flow of general shame and experience relief from all of its forms.

The following are some of the basic forms of shame:

Body shame. Our physical forms present many opportunities to admire or despise ourselves. Our fearfully, wonderfully made bodies are nevertheless flawed. Beyond those flaws, social comparison makes it possible for us to notice that we are not as big, strong, coordinated, athletic, or beautiful as someone else. Our culture can breed shame into us for simply being different from the idealized norm. Beyond this, some of us internalize negative messages and develop body dysmorphia in which a perfectly attractive person feels hideous.

Behavior shame. From being scolded as a schoolchild to getting a speeding ticket, we can feel shame over our behaviors. This is commonly called *guilt* when it pertains to specific deeds. But a more amorphous sense of being a bad boy or a bad girl would qualify as shame.

Mind shame. One's intelligence level can feed pride or shame, depending upon how a person measures against those within his or her world. Our academic system, with its focus on concrete forms of intelligence and its ranking of students through grading, can feed pride or shame and make or break a student's confidence.

Material shame. Poverty's greatest harm may be the sense of isolation that comes with it. Any time we have less than others, we can count on moments of cringing embarrassment when that becomes evident. The wealthy can also experience an isolating shame over their wealth.

Religious shame. Religion has distributed more shame than possibly any other force in modern society. In terms of Christianity, the moral standards are high and can cause feelings of never being good enough. Many sensitive souls have been chased out of the church by a sense of condemnation—both from the institution itself as well as the individuals within—that seems worse than hell itself.

Collective shame. It's possible to feel shame for one's family, church, community, nation, or another social group. We can and do feel ashamed of the decisions of our appointed leaders. We can also feel an involuntary shame reflex when our ethnic or religious group experiences or perpetrates discrimination.

Social shame. Body, behavior, and mind shame intersect with social shame in that we form our sense of self in the context of social comparison. Not feeling accepted and valued by others (that is, being unpopular) can crush the human spirit. We can also experience shame over relational failures, such as breakups, divorces, and estrangements; loneliness in and of itself can be a powerful purveyor of shame.

Shame versus guilt

Shame can be devastating in its effect. David prayed, "Let me not be ashamed" for a reason (Psalm 25:2)! Research associates shame with low self-esteem, hostility, social anxiety, depression, eating disorders, body dysmorphia, and a host of other psychological ills. Shame can spike stress levels, leading to other stress-related health issues. It can ravage the immune system, reducing our resistance to diseases of all kinds.

Guilt doesn't seem to have the negative impact of shame; even their respective definitions indicate the comparative severity of shame. Webster's dictionary defines *guilt* as "a feeling of deserving blame for offenses," while *shame* is "a condition of humiliating disgrace or disrepute."[6] Guilt says, "I did wrong," while shame says, "I *am* wrong." Guilt can stand up straight and take responsibility without a global sense of failure, whereas shame can't take responsibility because if I *am* wrong, I can do nothing *but* wrong.

Now let me throw a little wrench into the works. It's a wrench I have to introduce because to truly help resolve shame, I must be thorough in dealing with all aspects of it. Ready or not, here's my wrench: trying to shame away shame won't work. It's easy to take these basic facts of the harmfulness of shame and simply disallow it altogether. We have attempted that culturally as expressed in our slogans of "no shame" and "no regret," and we even have versions of it in church culture. In trying to help resolve spiritual shame, we tell people to stop being ashamed. Strangely enough, this moratorium on shame can actually increase it. I recall a counseling client relating a sermon she had heard in which the preacher proposed shame-free living. The client sobbed out her regret: "I shouldn't be ashamed, but *I still am*!" She had developed secondary shame, or shame about being ashamed. Since secondary disturbance forms a shell that prevents access to the primary disturbance, I address it first. I spent the next forty-five minutes helping my client to resolve the secondary shame so that we could access and impact her primary shame. My point is simply that disallowing shame isn't enough. Something has to step into the maelstrom of our shame spiral and restore sanity and self-respect.

In a 2014 study of the recidivism rates of 476 jail inmates, researchers discovered an interesting difference between shame and guilt. First, shame-prone inmates were more likely to reoffend than guilt-prone inmates. This makes sense, given that shame says, "I am all wrong and can do nothing but wrong," which precludes taking responsibility for one's crimes. Second, shame-prone inmates had a strong tendency to blame others for their crimes. That's not surprising either, given that the intense discomfort of shame can be temporarily mollified by passing it on to someone else. But—and here's the interesting part—the few shame-prone inmates that *didn't* blame others were no less likely to reoffend than the guilt-prone inmates. In fact, the authors of the study said, "The possibility that shame could be harnessed for social good is tantalizing."[7] Maybe, just maybe, if Adam and Eve had embraced their shame rather than resorting to blaming one another and God, they would have resolved it more quickly. It seems there's a healthy shame and an unhealthy shame. Healthy shame processing may nudge people toward moral change, but unhealthy shame cannot.

To get an idea of whether you are more prone to guilt or shame, see the "Guilt and Shame Inventory" in the toolbox. For a step-by-step, practical guide to busting feelings of shame, see "Shame Busters" in the toolbox.

Process versus product

I like to focus on the *process* of shame rather than the *product* of it. What matters isn't whether we have it or not—we all will at times if we have functioning consciences—but how we respond to it. In fact, because the universality of shame renders it unavoidable, I can't conscientiously tell people just to lose their shame; I would be setting them up for failure. But processed appropriately, shame can actually provide the first step in long-term change. God, in allowing us to possess the capacity for shame, hasn't assigned us to a cycle of shame and defeat but a process of allowing that shame to drive us to Him, where it can be released to One who loves us.

Shame, indeed, tells us that we *are* wrong. But aren't we? Comforting ourselves that we are really essentially good may anesthetize the pain for a time, but it can never treat its root cause. The human "heart is deceitful above all things, and desperately wicked" (Jeremiah 17:9). In response to a revelation of the holiness of God, we appropriately cry with Isaiah,

> "Woe is me, for I am undone!
> Because I am a man of unclean lips,
> And I dwell in the midst of a people of unclean lips;
> For my eyes have seen the King,
> The LORD of hosts" (Isaiah 6:5).

Some facts glare out from the Word of God, from the appalling annals of human history, and from our own self-knowledge—we are bent toward selfishness, sin, and ultimately, evil.

Left there, however, religious truth increases shame and ramps up its negative effects. "The letter kills" and "the law brings about wrath" (2 Corinthians 3:6; Romans 4:15). People die of shame and its ancillary emotions every day. Research on the relationship of religion and mental health show links between something called *punishing God reappraisals* and mental-health problems. "Punishing God reappraisals" simply means seeing traumatic events as punishments from God. In contrast, "benevolent religious appraisals" see God as good, even in the face of misfortune, and are linked with better mental health.[8]

Does this surprise us? "The goodness of God leads you to repentance" (Romans 2:4). Merely fearing God, we can *regret* our sins; we can even have *remorse* for them. But it's God's *goodness* as manifested through His sacrifice that enables us to *repent* of our sins. Repentance itself is a gift from God (Acts 5:31). As we see clearly the truth that Jesus "endured the cross, despising the shame," we find exactly the place where we can lay down our heavy burdens (Hebrews 12:2). He has already carried the shame we carry. It serves no divine purpose except to move us toward Him who melts our hearts in sweet sorrow.

Repentance heals; there is a holy worship that flows out of it. We don't need to remain in a guilt-ridden fixation on how we hurt Him; instead, we need to pass across that threshold to a place of utter safety in the arms of One who knows us completely and loves us just the same.

> Sometimes expressions hold half-hidden truth
> Like a rare orchid deep in a forest
> Like the lack that we show when we say "shame on you"
> When those words make the shamer the poorest.
>
> But that shame was indeed placed on One of great store
> Who bore all of our sin to reclaim us
> And receiving His gift, while it proves us as poor
> Tells the story that rendered us blameless.
>
> Shame on You, Jesus, shame on You
> Shame on the One to whom no shame was due
> Shame You despised and yet took to the tree where
> The shame was on You and the grace was on me.

DISCUSSION QUESTIONS

1. What evidence do we have that shame is a fundamental human emotion?

2. What examples of shame's pervasiveness do you see in human behavior?

3. What about shame triggers in us a tendency to blame others?

4. Shame prevents us from taking responsibility because if we *are* wrong, we _____.

5. Can we shame away shame? Why or why not?

6. What does healthy shame processing look like?

7. Is there anything good about shame? If so, what?

8. Share a time when the goodness of God led you personally to repentance.

9. Have you tended to see traumatic events as the judgments of God?

10. Has your religious experience fostered repentance or lingering shame? What needs to change?

---

1. Joseph Burgo, quoted in Lindsay Dodgson, "A Psychotherapist Says There Are 4 Types of Shame—Here's What They Are and How They Affect Us," *Business Insider*, April 3, 2018, https://www.businessinsider.com/different-types-of-shame-2018-3?r=UK.

2. Gershen Kaufman, quoted in Jane Bolton, "What We Get Wrong About Shame," Your Zesty Self, *Psychology Today*, May 18, 2009, https://www.psychologytoday.com/us/blog/your-zesty-self/200905/what-we-get-wrong-about-shame.

3. Anna Merritt, Daniel Effron, and Benoît Monin, "Moral Self-Licensing: When Being Good Frees Us to Be Bad," *Social and Personality Psychology Compass* 4, no. 5 (May 2010), https://doi.org/10.1111/j.1751-9004.2010.00263.x.

4. Daniel Effron, Jessica Cameron, and Benoît Monin, "Endorsing Obama Licenses Favoring Whites," *Journal of Experimental Social Psychology* 45, no. 3 (May 2009), https://doi.org/10.1016/j.jesp.2009.02.001.

5. Tom Porter, "Rothschild: Moral Outrage Can Be Self-Serving," Bowdoin College, March 6, 2017, https://www.bowdoin.edu/news/2017/03/rothschild-moral-outrage-can-be-self-serving.html.

6. *Webster's Third New International Dictionary*, Unabridged ed., s.vv. "guilt," "shame," accessed May 28, 2019, http://unabridged.merriam-webster.com.

7. June. P. Tangney, Jeffrey Stuewig, and Andres G. Martinez, "Two Faces of Shame: Understanding Shame and Guilt in the Prediction of Jail Inmates' Recidivism," *Psychological Science* 25, no. 3 (March 2014): 799–805, https://doi.org/10.1177/0956797613508790.

8. Russell Phillips III and Catherine Stein, "God's Will, God's Punishment, or God's Limitations? Religious Coping Strategies Reported by Young Adults Living With Serious Mental Illness," *Journal of Clinical Psychology* 63, no. 6 (June 2007): 529–540, https://doi.org/10.1002/jclp.20364.

Growth Mind-Set

My friend Pat Arrabito enjoyed her life as a mother of four young children and a wife to Jim—the love of her life. Poor in earthly goods but rich in affection, their daily lives were perfect in a crazy way. Pat homeschooled her brood of kids, who loved nature, art, science, reading, adventure, and well, life. In the evening, Jim would burst in the front door, grab Pat, and dip her back for a dramatic kiss. God had blessed both Pat and Jim with artistic ability, and they filled their home's walls with colorful paintings. They taught their children to support missions, which kept the family dreaming of people from faraway lands whom they hoped to meet someday.

One mission project took Jim and their two oldest children, Tony, who was thirteen, and Joey, eleven, to Alaska, where Jim would study the indigenous people for a video project. Tragically, their private plane crashed in the mountains. In the flames and rubble, Pat lost everything she held dear except her two youngest children, Adel and Andy.

I tear up now just thinking about how my friend carried on in the face of such loss. She raised her kids with love and discipline. She took the media ministry Jim had started and developed it into a production company putting out award-winning, multimillion-dollar films with household-name actors. She blessed countless lives with the fruits of her labor, casting beams of sunshine in many of the dark corners of this world, including mine. I call her "the counselor's counselor" because Pat is the person I call when I am shaken. She who has shed such bitter tears of loss has dried more tears of mine than I can count.

No one would fault Pat if she questioned God for allowing such a blow to come to a young wife and mother. I don't fault any who are doing that right now. But because she accepted the limits of her life on a planet kissed by death, she was "hard-pressed on every side, yet not crushed" (2 Corinthians 4:8). Pat expected much of God but only what He promised. She knew that God may not spare her suffering, but He could sustain her in it. Pat's realistic, biblical expectation of God is due to the fact that she survived and thrived in the face of unspeakable sorrow.

Expectations

According to scientific literature, a very interesting phenomenon called *active acceptance* has come forth as a key to coping with disappointments. "Active acceptance is an adaptive reaction to unchangeable situations" and is "positively related both to mental health and to behavior control." The researchers are quick to add that there's an unhealthy kind of acceptance called *resignation* that doesn't lead to mental health, and of course, nonacceptance causes problems too.[1] So let's define these three things in practical terms:

- *Nonacceptance*: "Something bad happened that never should have happened, and I will protest it by never accepting it."
- *Resignation*: "Something bad happened, and I can't do anything about it. It's hopeless."
- *Active acceptance*: "Something happened (which I don't like), but I don't expect a life without sorrow. What can I do next?"

Of course, the initial phases of grief involve all kinds of reactions that must be passed through before the acceptance stage. Elizabeth Kübler-Ross famously identified them as denial, anger, bargaining, and depression.[2] We would never walk in on a newly grieving widow like Pat Arrabito and say, "Just accept it, honey! Acceptance is good for your mental health." Acceptance after stubbing a toe might be instantaneous, but acceptance after losing one's husband and children—well, that will take some time. Playing the wrong chord at the wrong point in a song creates dissonance, but the chord isn't the problem, the timing is. We should never rush acceptance, but acceptance at the right time rings true and pure, reverberating hope and resiliency into our life's song. Pat says, "I just did what was in front of me when the sun came up every morning, hanging on to God for dear life, finding words that fit my need. And He did it. 'The one who calls you is faithful, and he will do it' " (1 Thessalonians 5:24, NIV).

How do we arrive at this healthy acceptance? Often, we must adjust our expectations to meet reality. Appropriate expectations of life set us up for contentment. When we expect a pretty life of uninterrupted pleasure and happiness, free of pain and struggle, we set ourselves up for a letdown of epic proportions. Of course, no one would admit to having such unrealistic dreams, but many, if not most, of us harbor them subconsciously and effectively operate out of them. Even believers, with their awareness of the world's fallen state and Jesus' promises of a better world to come, can continue to expect more out of temporal life than reality warrants. Out of this false expectation has sprung the prosperity gospel, which promises success and wealth if we only believe.

Once being materially blessed becomes the standard, those struggling with poverty and failure suffer not only from the material effects but also from a sense of having failed spiritually. This can marginalize the poor and struggling, shaming them away from the church. We feed this mentality in what we emphasize in our testimonies. We relate our earthly benefits: "God is so good! I got a raise, and now I will be able to pay for the addition to the house!" Rarely do we hear something like this: "I praise God that I lost my job. I was tempted with pride, and this will really help me become more like Jesus." In fact, church life tends toward a reward-centered Christianity, which always tends toward a temporal-reward focus. When we allow earthly blessings or their absence to tell us whether or not God loves us, we deprive ourselves of the sense of security in which God wants us to have constant rest.

Now, let me be fair. God does give us earthly tokens of His love. I don't want to make God seem apathetic to our joys and woes on earth. These things should provoke gratitude, not indifference: "Never one, saint or sinner, eats his daily food, but he is nourished by the body and the blood of Christ. The cross of Calvary is stamped on every loaf. It is reflected in every water spring."[3] Ultimately, these things point us to a heaven in which "God will wipe away every tear from . . . [our] eyes; there shall be no more death, nor sorrow, nor crying. There shall be no more pain, for the former things have passed away" (Revelation 21:4). More than this, they point to the loving character of a God who would make the ultimate sacrifice to take us to a better world.

As a freshman in college, I came to know Jesus. For the first time in my life, something filled the cavernous loneliness in my heart. I had learned of a God who loved me with an everlasting, unfailing, and unfathomable love. The love He had for me flowed from His innate goodness, yet at the same time, it was very distinctive. He knew me intimately and loved me personally. The richness of that connection to heaven seemed like the most precious thing I had ever stumbled upon, and I couldn't keep it to myself. Spilling over with joy, I went forth to "witness," and I lost every friend I had overnight. They didn't want to associate with the Jesus freak, and they let me know it in no uncertain terms. Humanly speaking, it was the loneliest experience of my life. At the same time, it was the sweetest experience of my life because into the space that earthly friends had left vacant came my heavenly Friend in all of His inimitable softness, warmth, and beauty. I often go back there in my memory just to relish the truth that while I lost earthly blessings to God, God beautifully stepped into the space of my loss.

In order to increase our capacity for joy, we must multiply the contexts in which we may experience it. If we only allow ourselves to be happy when earthly blessings fall, we greatly restrict our happiness and, interestingly, reduce those earthly blessings. God doesn't suddenly become stingy; through our limited gratitude, we reduce the space into which we can receive blessings. If we broaden the number of contexts in which we allow ourselves to be joyful, we broaden our hearts' capacities.

Reframing

Much of the day-to-day business of counseling and psychotherapy amounts to helping clients reframe their stories, showing how looking at a bad situation from a redemptive angle can change our entire perspective and experience. Nothing gives such reframing power as the gospel because it draws from an endless store of positives. The world can say, "You will grow from this," but so what? Why grow? Why not live out the adage "You can only be young once, but you can be immature forever"? Yet the gospel gives a solid motivation for growth. Placing personal growth in its context brings it alive with meaning. In that context, our growth contributes to the broader purpose of revealing the character of God in the universe: "We have been made a spectacle to the world, both to angels and to men" (1 Corinthians 4:9).

In reframing, we don't deny the difficulties or invalidate the distress that accompanies them, but we change our interpretation of them, effectively clearing a space for good to spring up in the muck of bad. Notice Jesus' masterful reframing: "Blessed are you when they revile and persecute you, and say all kinds of evil against you falsely for My sake. Rejoice and be exceedingly glad, for great is your reward in heaven, for so they persecuted the prophets who were before you" (Matthew 5:11, 12). In Jesus' day, His followers took their lives into their hands by professing Him. Through baptism, they put bounties on their own heads, and through preaching, they signed their own death warrants. The worst fate to befall a human being is death; it is the ultimate fear (Hebrews 2:15). Yet Jesus told these believers to rejoice in the face of persecution *because of what it meant.* It meant God held extra blessings in store for them. It meant they were on the right team. It meant they were serving a God of infinite love and that soon they would enjoy that love for eternity.

Paul learned the art of joy by using the gospel's power of reframing. The man who suffered imprisonment, whippings, and torture and who was beaten and stoned within an inch of his life learned to laugh in the face of death (2 Corinthians 11:16–27). "I know how to be abased, and I know how to abound. Everywhere and in all things I have learned both to be full and to be hungry, both to abound and to suffer need. I can do all things through Christ who strengthens me" (Philippians 4:12, 13).

Job, who in one flash of misfortune lost his children, his health, and the support of his wife, said,

"Naked I came from my mother's womb,
And naked shall I return there.
The Lord gave, and the Lord has taken away;
Blessed be the name of the Lord" (Job 1:21).

When his wife urged him to "curse God and die," Job responded, "You speak as one of the foolish women speaks. Shall we indeed accept good from God, and shall we not accept adversity?" (Job 2:9, 10). Notice that this man who personified courage in the midst of unspeakable suffering didn't expect God to protect him from all adversity. Nor did he hold back expressions of his pain. Job, seemingly the punching bag of Satan, "cursed the day of his birth" while scraping his boils and sitting in ashes (Job 3:1).

God never promised to protect us from all suffering. In fact, He promised the opposite: "In the world you *will* have tribulation" (John 16:33; emphasis added). But notice what comes forth in the next breath: "But be of good cheer, I have overcome the world" (verse 33). Jesus didn't deny the negatives, and neither should we. Positive thinking that disallows negatives unnaturally suppresses our normal human response to misfortune.

However, reframing processes those emotions by placing them in the context of the grand scheme of things, where they shrink in comparison to all the good that eternity can bestow upon us and can even be instrumental in increasing our capacity to enjoy that good.

Often, we look at our experiences in this sad, sinful, unfair world as reflective of God's heart. This is a pitfall we must avoid. As discussed in week 1, more than one supernatural will is active in this world. Though God reigns supreme, He does not remove all of the side effects that come with living on the front lines of the cosmic conflict. In the case of Jim Arrabito's plane, God didn't intervene to overthrow the laws of gravity, the reality of human error, and the basic, destructible nature of human flesh to keep Jim, Joey, and Tony alive. Pat chose not to see God's inaction as indifference, knowing that neither this world nor our experience in it accurately and comprehensively reflect God's heart toward us.

When we reject God's goodness based on the sad realities of life on earth, we argue from the wrong evidence. In life on earth, we encounter a mixture of God's blessings and the enemy's curses. This makes life on earth a cloudy window into God's character of love. How much better to go to a pure source of information. That pure source of information about God is available to us in the Cross. In reference to offering up His life for us, Jesus said, "Now the Son of Man is glorified, and God is glorified in Him" (John 13:31). Christ was essentially telling us, "Here's what God and I look like," and then pointing to the Cross, where He gave everything for our eternal happiness. That's a pure news source, right there. Everything that contradicts that is fake news about God.

To know God

With one cognitive shift, we can make our faith in God's goodness and our courage invincible. If we will move from believing the purpose of life is temporal happiness to believing our purpose is to know God, then nothing will discourage us. This doesn't mean that we shouldn't do all we can to secure happiness or that we should afflict our souls with bad experiences to help us grow spiritually. That would be fanatical and silly! However, the expansion of our spiritual lives, what we call growth, occurs in both enjoyable experiences and difficult ones; therefore, growth provides a driving motive that can never be frustrated.

We grow in both character and in love. Paul said he counted the things of this world as "rubbish" if He could have Jesus (Philippians 3:8). He stated his endgame as knowing "Him and the power of His resurrection, and the fellowship of His sufferings, being conformed to His death" (verse 10). Notice that knowing Christ had perks, such as resurrection power, and liabilities, such as sufferings. In other words, in the earthly context, there are pros *and* cons to following Jesus. In the eternal context, it's one big pro—to know Him. Notice as well the *quality* of the incentives. If we are looking for personal, temporal safety, following Jesus may disappoint. But if we are in it for love, if our all-consuming passion is to know God, following Jesus is a direct path to fulfillment.

We might shrink from this, realizing our shallowness, and wonder if we can possibly possess such far-reaching yet deep motivations. Let us not underestimate what God can do with the heart. God can deepen us. There's no essential difference between a martyr at the stake, praising Jesus as the flames consume his or her flesh, and us. He deepened the martyr's motives until all this person wanted was to know God, and He can deepen ours. With this purpose in place, we prefer suffering with Jesus to freedom from suffering without Him. Every experience teaches us, such that we have the secondary joy of fulfilling our purpose even when robbed completely of primary joy. Love is everything. When you are in love, even shared pain becomes an avenue to the heart's desire.

Can we experience joy and suffering simultaneously? Most definitely. The joy of the Lord doesn't whisk us away from the blood and guts of the human experience. It doesn't turn us into tearless Buddhas preaching detachment. Quite the opposite; it gives us just enough resiliency to experience our suffering fully so that our empathies stretch to their fullest. Without the joy of the Lord in the midst of suffering, we won't be able to bear it. We will turn to numbing addictions and distracting idols. But with God's joy to buoy us, we will plunge headlong into life with all of its pleasures and pains.

For a step-by-step guide, see "How to Know God" in the toolbox. For a tool to help you break common bad habits of thought and behavior, see "The Seven Deadly Psychological Sins Inventory" in the toolbox.

"Beloved, do not think it strange concerning the fiery trial which is to try you, as though some strange thing happened to you" (1 Peter 4:12). We are hated by an enemy. Through humans, demons, natural disasters, and diseases, the devil himself will try to crush our spirits. If our purpose in life is solely happiness and fulfillment, he will succeed, sooner or later. Don't go to social media, find a pretty life, and say, "But she has it all; why can't I?" That's an edited profile, not a life. Every child of God will meet with unspeakable sorrow and loss, if not before, then in death itself.

However, if we will receive from God that growth mind-set—that awareness that while He didn't promise us deliverance from suffering, He did promise growth through it and, ultimately, blessedly sweet growth in our love for and ability to be loved by Him—then *nothing* can defeat us. "We are more than conquerors" (Romans 8:37).

One day the Life-Giver will call Jim, Joey, and Tony Arrabito forth from the grave. I want to watch my beautiful friend Pat run into their arms for a long embrace.

DISCUSSION QUESTIONS

1. Share a time when you suffered because of unrealistic expectations.

2. In what ways have you tended toward nonacceptance or resignation?

3. What step could you take to engage in active acceptance of difficulties in your life?

4. Much of the religious world is obsessed with earthly happiness. What are some of the negative consequences of this?

5. In reframing, we don't deny the difficulties, but rather, _____ _____.

6. Who was the Master Reframer? Give a biblical example of reframing.

7. According to Paul, the greatest reward was to know God. How can God deepen our motives to that same point?

8. Why is life on earth a cloudy window into God's character of love?

9. Share a time when you experienced joy and suffering simultaneously.

10. With a growth mind-set, we grow both individually and in our relationships. How is God growing you in these ways?

---

1. Yuka Nakamura and Ulrich Orth, "Acceptance as a Coping Reaction: Adaptive or Not?" *Swiss Journal of Psychology* 64, no. 4 (2005): 281–292.

2. For more information on Elizabeth Kübler-Ross's model of the stages of grief, see Christina Gregory, "The Five Stages of Grief," Psycom, last updated April 11, 2019, https://www.psycom.net/depression.central.grief.html.

3. Ellen G. White, *The Desire of Ages* (Nampa, ID: Pacific Press®, 2002), 660.

Radical Security

When my mother broke the news that my father's company would be transferring our family to Milwaukee, Wisconsin, I buried my face in my hands and cried. The tears were prophetic. My childhood had been happy so far, with a nice house on a friendly block in a small town in Ohio where I had a close little circle of friends. All that would soon change.

"Mom, can I be buried in Aurora?" I sobbed.

"Well, of course," she said.

I dried my tears and prepared for a new life. Making new friends at Bayside Elementary School proved as treacherous as a mean-girl movie. The clique I tried to join used inclusion and exclusion to achieve dominance. Although this phenomenon bewildered my small-town-girl mind at the time, I get it now. It's human nature: being socially wired, we form groups; being naturally prideful, we try to make those groups "better than."

Henri Tajfel, a Polish-born British psychologist and pioneer of the social identity theory, recognized our tendency to form an in-group, making outsiders the out-group. These distinctions can involve race, culture, gender, age, religion, politics, and a host of other sources of identity. There is no harm in gravitating toward others with whom we have commonalities and forming groups around those commonalities, but things can become more complicated. For instance, one of the primary reasons people form groups is to improve self-esteem. In fact, people with lower personal self-worth tend to compensate for this by gaining self-worth from an in-group.[1] When they transfer their need for self-worth onto the group, they incentivize themselves to see their group in a positive light and outside groups in a negative light. Social scientists call these phenomena *in-group favoritism* and *out-group derogation*.

One of the most telling experiments on in-group and out-group psychology took place in the classroom of Jane Elliott, a teacher in Iowa. It was the day after the assassination of Martin Luther King Jr. in 1968. Elliott decided to address the problems of racial prejudice by dividing her third-grade class into groups on the basis of eye color. She proclaimed the blue-eyed children were superior to brown-eyed children, bestowing them with respective privileges and punishments: Blue-eyed children went out to recess; brown-eyed children stayed in. Blue-eyed children went to lunch first and could have seconds; brown-eyed children couldn't drink from the water fountain. In short order, the blue-eyed children turned into hate-mongers toward the brown-eyed children. They sadistically ridiculed their unfortunate classmates, calling them "stupid" and shunning them on the playground. "Brown eyes" became a derogatory term—a slur spoken with disdain. The next day Jane Elliott announced to the class: "Yesterday, I told you that brown-eyed people aren't as good as blue-eyed people. That wasn't true. I lied to you yesterday. The truth is that brown-eyed people are better than blue-eyed people." This produced the same result: the brown-eyed children became spitefully superior to the blue-eyed children.[2]

In-group and out-group dynamics lead to the formation of cliques. Clique formation in schools can be curbed if the schools actively facilitate desegregation, effectively forcing students to relate to out-group people. Some schools assign cafeteria seating once a month to alter students' social patterns.[3] But aside from the active countering of clique-formation dynamics, kids—especially adolescents, and particularly adolescents with low personal self-worth and sense of purpose—will harden into "better-than" groups.

Because the Bayside Elementary School mean girls were overall more attractive, funny, gifted, and intelligent, most students coveted membership in their clique. I was no exception. The mean girls toyed just enough with those outside their group to stay in the coveted category without actually including them. Then once in a while, they would escalate their exclusivism and attack some weak soul who wanted in but didn't quite measure up. One day my turn came. The mean girls drug me out to the baseball diamond, pushed me down, and made me wish I had never been born.

How ironic that during this period of bullying and abuse, the teachers assigned us to read *Lord of the Flies*, which is a book about a group of schoolboys who got stranded together on a deserted island and, over time, descended into savagery. They murdered two of their own, weaklings they thought beneath them, and nearly killed the protagonist Ralph before help finally arrived. The simultaneous reading of an in-group and out-group story, then bearing the brunt of that phenomenon in my own fragile self on the playground, forced me to face the basic cruelty of human nature.

Religious in-groups and out-groups

In-group and out-group psychology becomes very unsettling when combined with religion. In one study, "self-reported religiosity and spirituality correlated positively with more negative attitudes toward out-groups relative to in-groups." In a second study, the researchers found that subliminally priming individuals with religious terminology would lead to more out-group derogation.[4] In other words, when the researchers used religious terms, the participants' religious biases were triggered, and they became more pharisaical.

It's a sad fact that the very religion designed to prevent exclusivism actually seems to encourage it. However, it's not the religion of Jesus that causes such exclusivist behavior; it's the selfish insecurity of human nature imported into Christianity, where it garbs itself in religious-looking trappings. The religion of Jesus, as I hope to convey in the next few pages, carries a warm, inclusive, and generous message of God's heart of love to people. It draws a circle around people to count them in, rather than drawing a line to count them out. God has made an infinite sacrifice to adopt all human beings into His family while leaving us free to stay or not. Narrowness in Christianity is the result of the narrowness of human nature, not the narrowness of God.

We see an in-group and out-group phenomenon occurring in the early church regarding the circumcision of new believers. Some members, understandably confused about what to do with the Law of Moses but wedded to a certain religious exclusivism at the same time, hardened into a Judaizing clique. This created a social dynamic that completely contradicted the gospel of Jesus Christ.

In the book of Galatians, Paul fumes with anger over this, reserving his strongest language to call down the mean boys for their in-group attitude. Listen to his observation of the psychology behind it all: "They eagerly seek you, not commendably, but they wish to shut you out so that you will seek them" (Galatians 4:17, NASB). Shutting people out to achieve the thrill of being sought after and then rejecting the seekers to stoke up one's sense of superiority—that's the ugly, sinful human heart right there.

If we dig down a little, excavating the deep motives of the heart, we find a core of shame even in the most outwardly confident. People with narcissistic personality disorder will seem arrogant, proud, and entitled, but research has shown that they feel profound but largely subconscious shame.[5] They try to compensate for this shame through constant efforts to establish their superiority to others. A narcissist is characterized by a belief "that he or she is 'special' and unique and can only be understood by, or should associate with, other special or high-status people (or institutions)."[6] In a futile attempt to make themselves good enough, narcissists see others as not good enough. Narcissists create in-groups in a desperate attempt to compensate for their own sense of alienation from the in-group.

Narcissistic personality disorder can be diagnosed when one's narcissism becomes so prominent that it affects the ability to function in life and one's work and relationships. Because of our core of shame and sinful coping impulses, we all land somewhere on the narcissism spectrum. We form in-groups to try to compensate for the basic sense of alienation—never being good enough—that we all feel.

Alienation

We see our natural shame and alienation in Eden: Adam and Eve hide from God, accuse others, and just generally fall out of relationships into self-protection mode. We continue this pattern, adding insult to injury by blaming and shaming others and, ultimately, blaming and shaming God Himself. "The mind governed by the flesh is hostile to God; it does not submit to God's law, nor can it do so" (Romans 8:7, NIV). God describes us as "alienated from the life of God" and "alienated and enemies in your mind by wicked works" (Ephesians 4:18; Colossians 1:21). We are, "by nature children of wrath," "hateful and hating one another" (Ephesians 2:3; Titus 3:3). As sinful and selfish creatures, we have fallen profoundly, completely, and tragically out of love.

In order to save us from our narcissistic attempts to compensate for this alienation, we must experience a radical sense of inclusion. Our insecurities drive us toward compensatory narcissism. We can rail on the narcissist all day, but until the foundational insecurity is resolved, nothing will, or can, change.

Addressing our base insecurity is precisely what God did. In order to wean us of our self-absorption, He laid a foundation of secure inclusion in Christ. Understanding this radical security we have in Jesus changes our entire emotional landscape, ultimately unbending our inward, self-focused tendency and releasing us from fear-driven bondage into the freedom to love. Consider this passage:

> For when we were still without strength, in due time Christ died for the ungodly. For scarcely for a righteous man will one die; yet perhaps for a good man someone would even dare to die. But God demonstrates His own love toward us, in that while we were still sinners, Christ died for us. Much more then, having now been justified by His blood, we shall be saved from wrath through Him. For if when we were enemies we were reconciled to God through the death of His Son, much more, having been reconciled, we shall be saved by His life (Romans 5:6–10).

Let me distill this down to its essence, and you will see the sheer beauty of it: when we were without strength, sinners and enemies, we were reconciled to God through His Son.

Typically, reconciliation involves friends, but we were, according to this passage, enemies when it occurred. God did something life altering for us before we even had life. He reconciled the alienated parties, even when one party was still an enemy. He made us part of the ultimate in-group before we even asked.

The radical commitment of God

I had a conversation with my friend Brad about his girlfriend. "I am just not convinced she is committed to me," he said, "so I don't want to commit to her until I am sure." I think as soon as that came out of his mouth, Brad recognized the duplicity of what he said. Rather than requiring himself to commit to his girlfriend who was not committed to him, he was requiring his girlfriend to commit to him, even though he was not committed to her. Brad soon realized that someone would have to stop withholding commitment to end this cycle. He decided he would be the one, and he offered his girlfriend radical security in his love for her, whether she loved him back or not. I am not sure of the details, but they are married now with three beautiful kids, so it seems the risk paid off.

What if alienated humans were to learn that God is radically committed to them? That He cares primarily about building a relationship with them and only in that context about their belief systems and lifestyle choices? That He wants to know them on the heart level, thus creating an environment in the relationship that will facilitate the resolution of conflict between their souls and His? That He, the God of the cosmos, leans *toward* them in self-sacrificing love? That they are absolutely secure in that love?

This would be powerful, wouldn't it? Somehow Christianity has depicted God in a leaning-away posture, so abhorrent to sin that He can't stomach our weakness. Many believe that He holds Himself aloof, and even if sinners could make themselves holy enough to come into His presence, they would subject themselves to the scrutinizing eye of an all-seeing deity bent upon unearthing their every flaw. This image of God drives the sinful masses away from the gospel rather than drawing them toward it. Read this telling paragraph from the classic book *Steps to Christ* by Ellen White: "Satan led men to conceive of God as a being whose chief attribute is stern justice—one who is a severe judge, a harsh, exacting creditor. He pictured the Creator as a being who is watching with jealous eye to discern the errors and mistakes of men, that He may visit judgments upon them. It was to remove this dark shadow, by revealing to the world the infinite love of God, that Jesus came to live among men."[7]

Big, fat *but*

Now, it's true that God's standards are impossibly high. There is a dividing gulf between us. God is holy. He is just. We are sinful. If He were to allow sinful humanity into heaven, it would defile and derange His heavenly kingdom. But—and this is a big, fat, loud *but*—through Jesus' life, death, and resurrection, God did the work of reconciliation *within Himself* so that He could enter into a relationship with us *as we are*. We needn't make ourselves something we aren't, which is a good thing, given the fact that we can't change ourselves anyway. Jesus has done the work of reconciling God with humanity within His own divine-human being. With one arm, He embraced humanity, and with the other, He laid hold of the throne of God. We need only to see enough of His leaning-toward-love posture to realize He is trustworthy, and we will come to Him as we are. Jesus said, "Whoever comes to me I will never drive away" (John 6:37, NIV).

Without the baseline security of God's love, we can only be motivated by the fear of punishment or the hope of a reward. Those motives apart from deeper ones will taint all of our obedience with selfishness, rendering it sinful obedience. Security in His love disarms our self-protection and frees our motivational springs as God's love received flows back to

Him in worship and adoration. What comes next is true, Holy Spirit–infused obedience—real obedience from the heart.

Once we are established in a secure relationship with God, He will then lead us "in the paths of righteousness for His name's sake" (Psalm 23:3). How else could our fellowship with Him begin? How could we ultimately be made fit for a holy heaven? God crosses the impassable gulf, rather than urging us to try passing it ourselves. If we tried, we would only fall to our death in despair. Thank God that He comes forward with this message: I have reconciled you *already*. You are accepted, included, and adopted—you are in! Won't you please accept that status and follow Me?

In Christ

How did a holy God accept sinful humanity? Let us go back in time to get some illuminating historical context for God's great act of reconciliation. Getting the backstory brings more understanding to the present.

Even before our creation, God knew the risks involved, so He put in place a "counsel of peace" to save humankind in the event of a fall (Zechariah 6:13). At Creation, God gave humankind dominion over the earth—a dominion that Adam forfeited to the enemy when he partook of the forbidden fruit. Through sin, humanity lost its "right to the tree of life," symbolized in the fallen pair being driven from the Garden (Revelation 22:14). They had surrendered the rulership of the planet to "the prince of this world" (John 14:30, NIV). God honored Adam's decision to relinquish creation to an enemy; at the same time, He put in motion a covenant designed to restore creation. This covenant is simply God's promise to save humankind *within* Himself at any cost *to* Himself.

The covenant threads its way through the Bible narrative. We first see it in Genesis 3:15 when God promises to send a "Seed"—the biblical word for *descendant*—who would crush Satan's head. The idea resurfaces and expands in God's promise to Abraham to make him a "great nation" through his descendants (Genesis 12:2). Abraham fathered Isaac, who was the promised son and a type of Christ; Isaac fathered Jacob; Jacob fathered the twelve tribes, who became the nation of Israel, which God called "my firstborn son" (Exodus 4:22, NIV). Again and again, we see these sons as symbols of the Son of promise, Jesus. Through these symbolic sons, God is saying, "My Son is coming! Wait for Him!" And they did. Every Jewish woman hoped breathlessly that her son would be the promised Messiah.

Tumbling through a flawed genetic line, the promised Son, fathered by the Holy Spirit and mothered by the virgin Mary, appeared at the appointed time. But Jesus "came to His own, and His own did not receive Him" (John 1:11). They dogged His steps with persecution, finally delivering Him up to a Roman cross where He died by "God's deliberate plan and foreknowledge" (Acts 2:23, NIV). God moved through the chaos of human volition to bring about the fulfillment of His covenant in Jesus. Little did the actors know their freely chosen crimes against God actually played into His plan to save them.

> The very eyes that watched Him die
> were by the Savior lit.
> The very hands that drew His blood
> could kill because of it.

Through becoming one with us, taking on our fallen nature, Jesus qualified Himself to represent humanity as "the last Adam" (1 Corinthians 15:45). He then took that human nature to the cross, where He bore the divine penalty for sin, which is death (Romans 6:23). He used sinful human beings to carry out His will. Their sins put Him on the cross where their sins could be forgiven.

To a Jew, the cross meant the utter condemnation of the second death, past which no forgiveness or hope existed for the sinner. This symbol became fixed in their minds through their national history: God called Joshua to conquer Canaan, where the Canaanite kings knew of Israel's God and His miracles on behalf of His people: He parted the Red Sea, made water flow from a rock, sent manna from heaven, and defeated countless tribal armies on Israel's behalf. Through Abraham, these kings' forefathers had heard the gospel. Nevertheless, they corporately steeled their hearts against it and bred into their children the same rebellious spirit through the generations. Four hundred years after Abraham's rejected witness, Joshua defeated the kings and hung them on trees, leaving them until evening. Why? He wished to demonstrate how their persistent rebellion against God resulted in the forfeiture of heaven (Joshua 10:26). Under Israel's law, a criminal hanged on a tree was "accursed of God" (Deuteronomy 21:23).

Jesus' tormentors knew this story, they knew what hanging on a tree meant, and they wanted with all the passion of their hateful hearts to make that statement over His head.

The statement that "He is cursed of God" would hang in the air and saturate the very culture of Jerusalem, according to their plan. The most shocking aspect of the story, however, is not that Rome cooperated with their kangaroo court, but that *God* cooperated with it.

God Himself said, "He is cursed of God," because He was—on our behalf. Just sink down into that reality for a while, and let it soak into you. "Christ has redeemed us from the curse of the law, having become a curse for us (for it is written, 'Cursed is everyone who hangs on a tree')" (Galatians 3:13). Jesus—the Son of promise, God's Last Adam, and the glory of God who knew no sin—became sin that we might be made righteous through Him (2 Corinthians 5:21). "With perfect satisfaction Justice bowed in reverence at the cross, saying, It is enough."[8]

Having exhausted the demands of justice on our behalf, Jesus rested in the grave. On Resurrection morning, God called Him forth. Do you know who came with Him? You and I. "But God, who is rich in mercy, because of His great love with which He loved us, even when we were dead in trespasses, made us alive together with Christ (by grace you have been saved), and raised us up together, and made us sit together in the heavenly places in Christ Jesus" (Ephesians 2:4–6).

Did you notice that when "we were dead," God "made us alive together with Christ"? How? Some of us weren't even born yet! Being made alive couldn't have demanded our participation or even our existence. How, then, did God "make us alive"? By representing us as the Last Adam, the promised Messiah, the Son of the covenant. In Himself, He brought forth a new humanity, heirs of the new earth, a race who would regain everything lost to the first Adam and more. This passage doesn't apply primarily to our personal experience of being raised to a new life in Jesus, although that is a precious truth. This passage and others like it refer to an objective, historical fact that can't be altered by my choice to follow God or not. Because these truths are fully grounded in God's radical commitment to us, they form the basis of security for our relationship with Him.

> *Our hearts naturally crave inclusion, belonging, and being part of an in-group. We find that radical security in Jesus. For a tool that helps resolve conflict in the human realm, see the "AEIOU Conflict Resolution" in the toolbox. For a list of techniques that can help to calm us when we are highly emotional, see "Grounding Techniques" in the toolbox.*

"If then you were raised with Christ, seek those things which are above, where Christ is, sitting at the right hand of God. Set your mind on things above, not on things on the earth. For you died, and your life is hidden with Christ in God" (Colossians 3:1–3). Who died at the cross? You died. Who was raised? You were raised. "If One died for all, then all died" (2 Corinthians 5:14). "All" meaning the entirety of humanity. His death counts as ours.

Because He exhausted the divine penalty for sin and did it not only *for* us but *as* us and because He rose again as the Second Adam, humanity now stands free and clear of condemnation in Christ. And lest you think He did this for believers only, remember that He died for *enemies*. Is God "the God of the Jews only? Is He not also the God of the Gentiles? Yes, of the Gentiles also" (Romans 3:29). We need to understand God's love for His enemies because the truth is that even believers have a little bit of the enemy inside of them. Seeing God's radical commitment to and love for *all* people provides a basis for radical security for struggling believers. Perhaps a clearer focus on what God has done for the out-group will not only soften our hearts toward them but also fortify our own sense of belonging so that our egos are less invested in being part of an exclusive in-group. Then we can have a truly functional family with integrity, principles, and boundaries but also with a generous, inclusive love straight from the heart of God.

DISCUSSION QUESTIONS

1. What examples have you seen in your own life experience of in-group and out-group psychology?

2. How have you seen in-group and out-group psychology harm the spirituality of church circles?

3. Would you personally rather be part of a coveted in-group or a despised out-group? Why?

4. Why does the very religion designed to create inclusion sometimes foster unhealthy exclusivism?

5. Does your default mind-set have God leaning toward or away from you?

6. In what way is there an element of truth in the idea that God is too holy to accept us?

7. How did God resolve the dilemma of being too holy to accept humanity but too loving to destroy us?

8. Why did the enemies of Jesus want Him on a cross?

9. How did God make us part of the in-group of the heavenly family before we even existed?

10. Share a time when you felt like you belonged in a healthy, godly way.

---

1. Margareta Jelić, "Is Self-Esteem Predictor of In-Group Bias and Out-Group Discrimination?" *Review of Psychology* 16, no. 1 (2009): 9–18.

2. "Brown Eyes and Blue Eyes Racism Experiment (Children Session)—Jane Elliott," YouTube video, 14:36, July 24, 2016, https://youtu.be/KHxFuO2Nk-0.

3. Cindy Long, "Conquering Cliques in School," *NEAToday*, July 12, 2013, http://neatoday.org/2013/07/12/conquering-cliques-in-school/.

4. Megan K. Johnson, Wade C. Rowatt, and Jordan P. LaBouff, "Religiosity and Prejudice Revisited: In-Group Favoritism, Out-Group Derogation, or Both?" *Psychology of Religion and Spirituality* 4, no. 2 (May 2012): 154–168, https://psycnet.apa.org/doi/10.1037/a0025107.

5. Kathrin Ritter et al., "Shame in Patients With Narcissistic Personality Disorder," *Psychiatry Research* 215, no. 2 (February 2014): 429–437, https://doi.org/10.1016/j.psychres.2013.11.019.

6. American Psychiatric Association, "Narcissistic Personality Disorder," in *Diagnostic and Statistical Manual of Mental Disorders*, 5th ed. (Arlington, VA: American Psychiatric Association, 2013), 669.

7. Ellen G. White, *Steps to Christ* (Mountain View, CA: Pacific Press®, 1956), 11.

8. Ellen G. White, *Sons and Daughters of God* (Washington, DC: Review and Herald®, 1955), 243.

The Power of Belonging

Irvin Yalom grew up in a ghetto with Jewish immigrant parents. While they struggled to learn English and run a small grocery store, Irvin burrowed away in the apartment above the shop, reading everything he could find. An administrator from the local public school persuaded Irvin's parents to send their prodigy to a private school, which set him on an educational course that ultimately led him to earn an MD from Boston University School of Medicine. Possibly because of his deep desire for belonging as a Jewish child in a Gentile neighborhood or perhaps in reaction to the emotional abuse of his mother, Yalom became the best-known expert on group therapy in the world. (His book *The Theory and Practice of Group Psychotherapy* is about four inches thick.)

Group meetings are powerful. Group therapy has been used since the early 1900s to treat a variety of issues: posttraumatic stress, depression, grief, loneliness, and a host of other specific problems, such as eating disorders or phobias. The twelve-step movement began in 1935 with two alcoholics—now affectionately known as "Bill W." and "Dr. Bob"—using group meetings as the basis for an addiction-recovery program that has literally saved millions of people. Group meetings generally involve sitting in a circle, which is a metaphor for the team approach to helping people thrive.

One of the benefits of group therapy that Irvin Yalom identifies is "the corrective recapitulation of the primary family experience."[1] This refers to the overwriting of flawed bonding experiences in one's family of origin. Our developmental process literally wires our brains, creating synaptic pathways of healthy bonds, unhealthy bonds, broken bonds, or in most of our cases, a mixture of all three. We learn many of our beliefs and behaviors in a preconscious or nonverbal way through imitating behaviors, absorbing the thinking of those around us. In our brokenness, we bring the same dysfunctional patterns into our adult relationships, and unless we learn new ways of relating to others, we will continue to perpetuate the past. Group therapy purports to have the power to reform these patterns and pathways, taking us back to similar dynamics within the group "family" but with good leadership and healthy norms leading us into conflict resolution rather than escalation or avoidance, belonging rather than rejection or enmeshment, and group cohesion rather than relational brokenness.

The stages of group therapy have been described with a high degree of accuracy as *forming*, *storming*, *norming*, *performing*, and *adjourning*.[2] Here's how things typically roll out: After the initial formation stage comes the storming, characterized by conflict as each member tries to establish his or her role and dominance level in the group. During this stage, the leader, heretofore honored and respected, falls from grace. Storming becomes one big conflict free-for-all; experienced therapy group leaders warn that without sufficient guidance and group norms, storming can destroy the group entirely. With proper leadership and norming, or standards of conduct and procedure, the group can start performing as a unit where each individual finds acceptance and belonging. It is then that the "corrective recapitulation of the primary family experience" can take place. People can feel, often for the first time in their lives, accepted by others, and their group is a family of sorts.

Social acceptance

Social acceptance makes us better people. In two experiments, C. Nathan DeWall, a psychology professor from the University of Kentucky, found that the social acceptance levels of the participants negatively correlated with aggression levels; in other words, the more accepted the participants felt, the less aggressive they were. Here's how the experiments worked: The participants had various numbers of people acting either in an accepting or nonaccepting way toward them. Then the researchers staged opportunities for the participants to act aggressively. In the first experiment, they could require an innocent stranger to eat a very spicy hot sauce, and in the second, they could shock an innocent stranger with a very loud noise.

The results were unmistakable. In every case, the greater the number of accepting people, the lower the participant's aggression levels.[3]

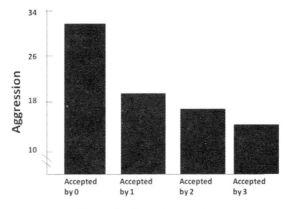

Figure 1. Experiment 1.

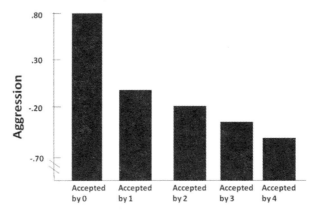

Figure 2. Experiment 2.

Notice especially the large gap between 0 and 1. This means acceptance by just *one* person nearly *halved* the aggression levels of the participants.

As children, my friend Kate and I spontaneously performed a little social experiment of our own on her younger brother Timmy. Most days Timmy plagued us with his bratty, little-brother antics. We treated him like the pond scum we thought he was, and he didn't disappoint. But one day in a flash of inspiration, Kate and I decided we would treat Timmy differently. We would honor and respect him, including him in our tree fort and make-believe world. Timmy became a different person. He cooperated and shared, drawing even more affirmation from us until at the end of the day we decided to make him a little tinfoil crown and enthrone him as the prince of the house.

The church and belonging

The urge to belong, be accepted, be included, and even be loved by others is as basic to human nature as the need for food and water. Jesus' body of believers is called by God to speak to this need powerfully. The Greek word *koinonia* conveys the idea that in Jesus Christ, we have just such an inclusive unit. Human beings are one in Jesus because He "has broken down the middle wall of separation" between people (Ephesians 2:14).

Koinonia comes from the Greek *koinos*, which means "common" and "ordinary." New Testament writers expanded it into a term that specifically means Christian fellowship.

> We proclaim to you what we have seen and heard, so that you also may have fellowship with us. . . .
>
> . . . If we walk in the light, as he is in the light, we have fellowship with one another, and the blood of Jesus, his Son, purifies us from all sin (1 John 1:3, 7, NIV).

Koinonia is fellowship, sharing, communion, and the oneness of a social group; this is similar to *group cohesion* in group therapy. God calls us to be adopted into His family (Ephesians 1:5). We experience, to a greater or lesser extent, natural love within our birth families but supernatural love within the family of God. And within this supernatural family, each member can experience *corrective recapitulation*, or the rewriting of our relational history. In other words, the church is God's therapy group; because of the social acceptance and secure bonds we enjoy there, we can all become our best selves.

I know some of you are scoffing right now, having experienced petty judgmentalism and pharisaical exclusivity, not acceptance, in church. I empathize with those who have been burned by the church, having been scorched myself a few times. Yet I can't help but uphold the ideal. I wonder what would happen if the church became an extremely welcoming place where social acceptance abounded and love spilled over the edges to bathe the world.

Oh, wait! That's what is supposed to happen.

Now, to be fair and balanced, the church is called to separate from the world: "Come out from among them and be separate, says the Lord" (2 Corinthians 6:17). In the light of Jesus we experience a unique fellowship (1 John 1:7). Jesus calls us to be *in* the world but not *of* it. When the church loses its distinctiveness, its purpose, and its power to provide refuge for those burned by the world, it loses its effectiveness in reaching the world.

But the foundational distinction between the church and the world is a gospel distinction. Since the beginning, the difference between believers and nonbelievers has been obvious: by offering an animal sacrifice, Abel honored the gospel of trusting in the merits of the coming Messiah; but Cain dishonored it, trusting in himself, and his self-righteous religion ultimately fueled the hateful murder of his brother. From Genesis, we follow the thread of the two spiritual systems—self-salvation and salvation by faith—till their culmination in Revelation. In Revelation, we find the world split into two camps: those following the man-made, man-trusting religion of the beast, and those trusting in the merits of the slain Lamb.

God calls the followers of Jesus together into a body of people tasked with demonstrating the gospel to the world, and the distinctiveness of God's message empowers the church to carry forth this mission. The unique principles of God's kingdom sharply contrast with the principles of the world. Through witnessing that contrast, seekers get a glimpse of the gospel: "By this all will know that you are My disciples, if you have love for one another" (John 13:35). The church sometimes practices forms of pseudoacceptance that threaten its purity, along with its very mission, but when the loving acceptance of all of God's children as human beings made in His image and purchased by His blood retains its tone, it empowers great things.

Separatism

In the hands of prideful human beings, separateness can deviate into separatism—religious exclusivism in which, even while the church appears holy, the world's principles of selfishness come in through the back door. Just as Israel of old, the church can separate from the world's *people* instead of its *principles*. After Jesus' resurrection, the Holy Spirit opened the door for the Gentiles, causing some Jews to recoil in reflexive horror, leading Paul to plead, "Is God the God of Jews only? Is he not the God of the Gentiles too? Yes, of Gentiles too" (Romans 3:29, NIV). We need the same reminder today. See all of those people out there who believe things and do things you would never believe or do? God is their God too;

they just don't know it yet! And guess what? You are supposed to tell them. "But you are a chosen generation, a royal priesthood, a holy nation, His own special people, that you may proclaim the praises of Him who called you out of darkness into His marvelous light" (1 Peter 2:9).

Through His death and resurrection, Jesus united humanity with God. He also united humanity with each other; specifically, He made fellowship in His body accessible through the door of faith. At any instant, an unbeliever can exercise the "measure of faith" God has given to "each one" and in that moment transition from the kingdom of the world into the kingdom of God (Romans 12:3).

We see a flood of spontaneous faith awakenings in the closing scenes of Jesus' life. Simon of Cyrene carried Jesus' cross, forced by Roman soldiers at first but then from a cheerful choice to follow Him (Mark 15:21). The thief on the cross expressed faith; Jesus told him he would also be in paradise (Luke 23:43). The Roman soldiers said, "This was the Son of God!" (Matthew 27:54). Jesus still walks among us today through the Holy Spirit. If at any given moment, a soul responds positively to the witness of the Spirit, in that instant, this person is just as much a believer as those who have occupied church pews for decades. And we have the privilege of seeing this individual as such. In Jesus, God has removed the barrier between ourselves and the unbelieving world, opening up the avenue of faith for those seeking asylum.

> But now in Christ Jesus you who once were far off have been brought near by the blood of Christ.
>
> For He Himself is our peace, who has made both one, and has broken down the middle wall of separation (Ephesians 2:13, 14).

Two reactions

God's radical acceptance of each human being, which is called *love*, is accompanied by a radical hatred of anything that would harm a human being, which is called *sin*. How can a mother love her child and not hate what hurts her child? How can God love us without hating sin? The two are inextricably bound together, and any attempt to separate them will destroy both.

People respond in one of two ways to this truth: one class will feel loved by God, interpreting His hatred of sin as a jealousy for their souls, and the other will feel hated. The simple factor distinguishing these two experiences is identity. When individuals identify with sin, they will experience God's rejection of sin as a personal rejection. Nothing in God changes toward them—He is love, and He loves and accepts them unchangingly. What determines the sense of rejection is that these people have identified themselves by something God abhors, which creates within their own hearts a filter that darkens the truth of God's radical acceptance.

This makes the formation of a new identity a life-or-death issue. Jesus taught that in order to "see the kingdom of God," one must be "born again" (John 3:3). In that born-again experience, a temporary destabilization of one's identity occurs, leading to a resettling of a new identity as a believer in Christ. This restructuring of identity can be uncomfortable, even harrowing. But the final product brings serenity and peace as the result of a conscious sense of God's acceptance.

Research shows that those who identify with their faith group experience more well-being in religious activities.[4] In other words, identity can make or break us religiously and spiritually. People attend church (God's building) out of a sense of duty; they *become* "God's building" when carried along by a sense of affinity with the Builder (1 Corinthians 3:9). In fact, the church isn't a building or an event so much as it's a fellowship of human beings who have identified themselves as followers of Jesus Christ.

The church's task in the Great Commission is not just to herd people into the church building but to help them realize their place in Christ. Jesus already sees them as His own children and as members of the earthly family He created by His power and saved by His blood. But they don't yet see themselves that way. What agencies does the Spirit use to awaken in them an awareness of who they really are? Well, He uses other struggling human beings—believers. We can find a key to this process in the writings of Paul:

For Christ's love compels us, because we are convinced that one died for all, and therefore all died. And he died for all, that those who live should no longer live for themselves but for him who died for them and was raised again.

So from now on we regard no one from a worldly point of view. Though we once regarded Christ in this way, we do so no longer. Therefore, if anyone is in Christ, the new creation has come: The old has gone, the new is here! All this is from God, who reconciled us to himself through Christ and gave us the ministry of reconciliation: that God was reconciling the world to himself in Christ, not counting people's sins against them. And he has committed to us the message of reconciliation (2 Corinthians 5:14–19, NIV).

Notice that because One died for all, all died. God doesn't squint down at the masses of humanity, demanding payment for their sins. He already met the just demands of the law in His own body on a lonely cross. We embody God's liberality when we also "regard no one from a worldly point of view," refusing to identify them with their earthly, sinful selves, instead, identifying them with their "new creation" status in which old things have passed away. When we look at people, do we see their best selves or their worst selves? God would like to infuse His people with the spirit of interpersonal generosity, identifying people as their best selves, even if that best self hasn't yet been realized.

Have faith in people

Have you ever experienced the potent rush of motivational power that springs from a person having faith in you? There is nothing like it! Author Ellen White said, "If we wish to do good to souls, our success with these souls will be in proportion to their belief in our belief in, and appreciation of, them. Respect shown to the struggling human soul is the sure means through Christ Jesus of the restoration of the self-respect the man has lost. Our advancing ideas of what he may become is a help we cannot ourselves fully appreciate."[5]

One of the greatest hindrances to the church instilling faith in people is the politicization of Christianity. Politics create polarities in which those outside of our political perspective become enemies instead of potential friends. We lose the spirit of the Great Commission when we see political opponents as enemies. Caught up in the polarities of the world, we can even begin to need the world to be wrong to prove the rightness of our political pet rock. The systems of the world, including political systems, are "under the control of the evil one" (1 John 5:19, NIV). God is calling people to leave those systems. He cries, "Come out of her, my people" (Revelation 18:4, NIV). Will they find a safe place?

Much of the reason we lack emotional generosity toward others is because we fail to see God's generosity toward us. So many deeply religious people have what in psychology is called an *anxious attachment style* to God. We become sensitive to rejection, as do badly parented children. If only we would remain aware of the reality of God's generous acceptance of us, which He extended even when we were enemies, then we would find an invincible, insuppressible joy that would spill over the borders of our faith community onto the parched earth surrounding it.

The "faith of Jesus" (see Revelation 14:12) may be understood as "faith in Jesus," which works theologically and exegetically. But it may also be understood as Jesus' faith in us. Some balk at the idea of an all-seeing God possessing faith, but the Bible actually says He's *full* of faith—as in faith*ful*. In fact, the chief Old Testament word for divine love, *chesed*, can mean "faithfulness." *Faith* can mean to have confidence; to have faith in someone means to have confidence in them. I don't know how God can see the future of those who will ultimately rebel against Him and still have confidence in them, but I do know that their rebellion won't be because of any doom speaking on His part. And think about it. If God says that you are going to fail, well, who can resist the power of that thought? Rather, He tells humanity, "I died to create a new humanity and brought that new humanity forth from the grave with Me. I hold in My heart a picture of you redeemed, made new, fully surrendered to your destiny as a subject of My kingdom. I have given you agency, volition, a free will to choose that destiny, and I envision you making that choice." God puts every available bit of psychological machinery in place to urge us toward His plan for us, maximally incentivizing our choice to follow Him without reservation. If we could grasp this for ourselves and share it with others, then the church would become a powerful source of spiritual, emotional, and relational healing in the world.

Consider a few facts:

- *Worldly people are fellow heirs of God's kingdom*: "The Gentiles should be fellow heirs, of the same body, and partakers of His promise in Christ through the gospel" (Ephesians 3:6).
- *God has already reconciled worldly people to Himself*: "For it pleased the Father that in Him all the fullness should dwell, and by Him to reconcile all things to Himself, by Him, whether things on earth or things in heaven, having made peace through the blood of His cross" (Colossians 1:19, 20).
- *God has shown Himself to worldly people in Jesus*: "For the grace of God has appeared that offers salvation to all people" (Titus 2:11, NIV).

- *God redeemed worldly people of every ethnicity, culture, and nation*: "For You were slain, and have redeemed us to God by Your blood out of every tribe and tongue and people and nation, and have made us kings and priests to our God; and we shall reign on the earth" (Revelation 5:9, 10).

> *For help with changing the most common bad habits in relationships, see "The Seven Deadly Relationship Sins Inventory" in the toolbox. For a helpful conflict-resolution tool, see "AEIOU Conflict Resolution" in the toolbox.*

- *The Cross reversed the condemnation of worldly people*: "Therefore, as through one man's offense judgment came to all men, resulting in condemnation, even so through one Man's righteous act the free gift came to all men, resulting in justification of life" (Romans 5:18).

DISCUSSION QUESTIONS

1. How has the family of God provided you with a "corrective recapitulation of the primary family experience"?

2. Can you think of a time when you became your best self because you felt accepted?

3. God's love, in order to be love, must hate what harms the objects of His love. What in your life does He hate?

4. What happens to our sense of God's love for us when we identify with sin?

5. Who in your life has believed in you, and how have they shown it?

6. Whom have you believed in, and how have you shown it?

7. What happens when the faith of Jesus becomes politicized?

8. What emotions do you feel when you see God's deep emotional generosity toward all humanity?

9. How can you better reveal that emotional generosity to those around you?

10. We all want to belong, but sometimes we resist it. What about belonging scares or otherwise puts you off?

1. Irvin Yalom, *The Theory and Practice of Group Psychotherapy* (New York: Basic Books, 1970), 77.

2. Bruce Tuckman, "Developmental Sequence in Small Groups," *Psychological Bulletin* 63, no. 6 (1965): 384–399, https://psycnet.apa.org/doi/10.1037/h0022100.

3. C. Nathan DeWall et al., "A Little Acceptance Goes a Long Way: Applying Social Impact Theory to the Rejection-Aggression Link," *Social Psychological and Personality Science* 1, no. 2 (2010): 198–174, https://doi.org/10.1177/1948550610361387.

4. Emily A. Greenfield and Nadine F. Marks, "Religious Social Identity as an Explanatory Factor for Associations Between More Frequent Formal Religious Participation and Psychological Well-Being," *International Journal for the Psychology of Religion* 17, no. 3 (2007): 248–259, https://www.ncbi.nlm.nih.gov/pmc/articles/PMC2507864/.

5. Ellen G. White, *Fundamentals of Christian Education* (Nashville, TN: Southern Pub. Assn., 1923), 281.

Posttraumatic Growth

As tour guide Kay Wilson crawled through a forest near Jerusalem on December 18, 2010, bleeding from thirteen stab wounds—also suffering "punctured lungs and diaphragm, [a] dislocated shoulder, broken shoulder blade, and a broken sternum"[1]—she filled her mind with music. As a jazz musician, Kay could compose in her head. What better time to create an arrangement of "Somewhere Over the Rainbow" than while bleeding out and fighting for her life? The juxtaposition of trauma and triumphant song is a perfect metaphor for Kay Wilson's character and experience.

Ayad Fatafta and Kifah Ghanimat, two members of a Palestinian terror cell wielding a long, serrated knife, had attacked Kay and her friend Kristine Luken. Kristine died. Because Kay played dead convincingly enough for the terrorists to leave, she lived. She had stabbed one of the attackers with a penknife, and the authorities were able to trace the DNA to the killers. The community declared Kay a heroine.

What may be more heroic than her effort to fight back was Kay's means of processing the trauma. She has become a case study of the phenomenon called *posttraumatic growth*, identified by social scientists as a positive coping mechanism that can literally make or break a person after a traumatic event. Posttraumatic growth (PTG) basically changes the narrative that trauma ruins people into something more hopeful and redemptive. But PTG researcher Lawrence Calhoun cautions that "the presence of posttraumatic growth will not, necessarily, result in an equivalent reduction in distress."[2] The person experiencing PTG suffers from the trauma just as intensely as the one who doesn't experience PTG; however, one person grows from it, and the other doesn't.

The story of trauma, as told by the world we live in, recounts the following message loud and clear: "Trauma is bad. It ruins you. Avoid it at all costs." Given that much of the most devastating trauma occurs when we have no ability to escape it, this seems quite cruel. In fact, one of the things that causes the damage of trauma is the inescapability factor, which leads to *depersonalization* (feelings of detachment from self) and *derealization* (feelings of detachment from the world). In other words, people who can't physically escape a dangerous situation will try to escape psychologically. However, this can affect their ability to function. Could we, by promoting the message that trauma ruins people, unintentionally extend that inescapability factor into the future? To tell people at their most helpless point that they sustained permanent damage is to give trauma a huge amount of power.

Trauma is part of the story. It's not the whole story.

Trauma is real

Let me begin with the trauma portion of the story, without undercutting the extremity of it in an effort to find a quick solution. It can be very healing to hear another person acknowledge one's trauma; it can validate and normalize what feels frightening and unpredictable.

Posttraumatic stress disorder (PTSD) is an official diagnosis in the *Diagnostic and Statistical Manual* (DSM) of the American Psychiatric Association. PTSD is acquired by directly experiencing or witnessing a traumatic event. To qualify for a diagnosis, the trauma must come from "exposure to actual or threatened death, serious injury, or sexual violence."[3] The disorder presents with recurrent, involuntary, and intrusive distressing memories of the event. These typically come in the form of flashbacks, nightmares, and extreme sensitivity to triggers. The traumatized person will often engage in life-altering avoidance of triggers. People with PTSD can become chronically anxious, reactive, irritable, and hypervigilant. The patterns develop into "clinically significant distress or impairment in social, occupational, or other important areas of functioning."[4]

Complex posttraumatic stress disorder (C-PTSD) is a psychological disorder that occurs as a result of repetitive, prolonged trauma involving sustained abuse or abandonment by a caregiver or other relation with a power advantage. C-PTSD didn't make it into the fifth edition of the DSM as a stand-alone diagnosis; nevertheless, it is considered a real phenomenon.

Adverse childhood experiences (ACE) are stressful or traumatic events experienced in childhood, typically over a long stretch of time as in C-PTSD. They include physical abuse, sexual abuse, emotional abuse, physical neglect, emotional neglect, witnessing intimate partner violence, substance abuse in the home, mental illness in the household, parental separation or divorce, an incarcerated house-hold member, and other distressing events.

For help coping with the effects of PTSD or other anxiety, see "Grounding Techniques" in the toolbox. For help with calming a raw nervous system, see "Relaxation Technique" in the toolbox.

The ACE study

There's a fascinating story behind the study that led to the coining of the term *adverse childhood experiences*. In the 1980s, Dr. Vincent Felitti, the head of Kaiser Permanente's Department of Preventative Medicine in San Diego, noticed that 55 percent of the participants dropped out of their weight-control clinic. *Almost all of them have been losing weight. Why are they leaving?* he wondered. Felitti conducted interviews with 286 people who had left the program. The turning point of his quest to understand the dropout phenomenon came by accident. He was asking one woman routine questions:

How much did you weigh when you were born? In first grade? In high school? . . .

"I misspoke," he recalls. "Instead of asking, 'How old were you when you were first sexually active,' I asked, 'How much did you weigh when you were first sexually active?' The patient, a woman, answered, 'Forty pounds.' "

He thought he'd misheard. He asked again. She gave the same answer, began sobbing, and added: 'It was my father.' "

Felitti had only run into one case of incest in his entire medical career, so he felt flustered and unsure of what to do. Again and again, in his interviews with the weight-loss program dropouts, he heard similar stories. He says, "It seemed that every other person was providing information about childhood sexual abuse."

He met one woman who had been raped at twenty-three and had gained 105 pounds in the year after the attack. She looked down at the floor and said, "Overweight is overlooked, and that's the way I need to be."

He realized that weight gain can be a coping mechanism for depression, anxiety, and fear in people who have experienced sexual trauma. This explains why the patients dropped out of the program, even though they were losing weight. It was *because* the program worked that they left. Faced with the loss of their coping strategy, they didn't *want* to lose weight.

Teaming up with an epidemiologist from the Centers for Disease Control and Prevention, Felitti surveyed more than seventeen thousand Kaiser Permanente patient volunteers about their childhood trauma. Most of the participants reported at least one adverse childhood experience. The ACE Pyramid came forth from that study. It shows the clear cause-and-effect relationships of ACEs to social, emotional, and cognitive impairments; the adoption of high-risk behaviors; disease, disability, and social problems; and finally, early death.[5]

So there you have it. Trauma is real, and its effects are crushing. Childhood trauma, which occurs before the rational, reasoning part of the brain develops, devastates the worst. I want to validate up front what trauma victims have been through. Denying it is futile; it will wake us up at night. Invalidating it will only increase the distress. Issuing religious-sounding platitudes will mock the pain. Prescribing more prayer or Bible study is often religious people's attempt to escape the discomfort of empathy. Trauma sits in our nervous system like a big, fat, ugly sore, ready to bleed at the slightest provocation.

Labeling

I love it when I can label something for people. They come, saying, "My dad didn't try to kill me or sexually abuse me. It's just that he . . . never talked to me, and when he did, he was always irritated and critical. He raged at mom a lot and drank himself into a stupor every night."

I say, "That's called complex posttraumatic stress disorder, or C-PTSD. It's the result of repetitive, prolonged trauma that can come through neglect or being raised in an unsupportive, chaotic environment. It doesn't come from one big, catastrophic event so much as repeated microevents. It's like when I tap on your arm; it doesn't hurt unless I do it for three days straight. That's how C-PTSD works. It's not just *what* happened; it's how *often* it happened."

They say, "Really? It's a thing?"

"It's a thing," I say. "You're not alone."

The relief that comes when they realize that their condition isn't the result of a moral failure or an incurable disease makes all the drawbacks of the label tolerable. I realize the pitfalls of labeling and diagnosis, but it has its place, and sometimes its place is to begin the healing process through validation. When we *define* something, we *confine* it and make it less pervasive, which, in the case of someone whose trauma response has taken over his or her life, can be very therapeutic.

The contrast

Let me share with you a bit of my own journey concerning how to regard trauma and its effects. I'm a student of psychology, a reader of scientific studies, but also a believer in the Bible. I saw two different pictures of trauma that eventually came together into a more complete picture as I continued to search. Science has done a good job of defining the problem of trauma. Defining it can help as a first step. But as I wrestled through it, I found myself wanting to look at trauma from a more redemptive angle.

So naturally, I turned to the Redeemer.

The Bible abundantly affirms trauma and its effect. The story of Amnon and Tamar from 2 Samuel 13 leaps out as a case study. David's many wives produced a large, complex household. Prince Amnon lusted after his half-sister Tamar. So overcome with desire was he that he became depressed and began to lose weight. His friend Jonadab told him to feign illness and have David send her to his house. Following David's instruction, Tamar arrived at his home and fixed a meal for him. "But when she took it to him to eat, he grabbed her and said, 'Come to bed with me, my sister' " (verse 11, NIV). For a woman in that day to lose her virginity rendered her unfit for marriage, so Tamar begged Amnon to "speak to the king; for he will not withhold me from you" (verse 13). Instead, he violently raped her. Then, like a true psychopath, he was repulsed and disgusted by his victim. "Be gone!" he roared (verse 15).

In true ancient Near Eastern form, Tamar doused her pretty head with ashes, tore her multicolored princess robe, and fled to her full brother Absalom's house, where she remained "desolate" for the rest of her life (verse 20). The Hebrew word for "desolate" is *shamem* and has a verb form that means "to numb," "to stun," "to devastate," and "to stupefy."

King David knew about Amnon's crime but did nothing, inflicting a secondary trauma of neglect. After the rape, Tamar is never mentioned again. Perhaps she dies, we don't know; but a few years later Absalom fathers a beautiful daughter and names her—you guessed it—Tamar (2 Samuel 14:27). Was it in memory of his sister? In one way or another, she had died.

Now there's a story of the devastating effects of trauma!

Rejoice

As I look at what the Word of God says about these shattering experiences, I see something that contrasts with the desolate state of Tamar. I see believers in the true God somehow thriving in spite of their own horrifying distresses.

I see Noah and his family rebuilding their lives after a worldwide flood.

I see Abraham surviving the death of his brother and near death of his own son.

I see Moses enduring the plagues of Egypt and a life of wilderness wandering.

I see David writing beautiful poetry about running for his life.

I see Jehoshaphat's army singing in the face of military onslaught.

I see the enslaved, deported, and probably castrated Daniel thriving as an intellectual leader in Babylon.

I see Mary Magdalene busting through sexual and social trauma to create a beautiful portrait of the Cross.

I hear the persecuted Paul say, "We are hard-pressed on every side, yet not crushed; we are perplexed, but not in despair; persecuted, but not forsaken; struck down, but not destroyed" (2 Corinthians 4:8, 9). "Our light and momentary troubles are achieving for us an eternal glory that far outweighs them all" (verse 17, NIV).

Many of these hard-pressed, perplexed, persecuted, and struck-down people lived with the constant threat of assault and even martyrdom; they were often brought before kings and queens to plead for their lives; and they were misunderstood by their own people. But they thrived in spite of it. Jesus had said, "Rejoice and be glad, because great is your reward in heaven," and they rejoiced (Matthew 5:12, NIV).

Is it possible to process trauma in such a way that the energy of it ultimately fuels joy? Could trauma benefit us, if not in the short term, in the long term? While it may not improve our quality of life, could it improve the quality of our characters? These stories seem to indicate that even though the devastating effects of trauma are *part* of the story, they're not the whole story.

As I mulled over the contrast between the "trauma is the end of the story" script and the "trauma is only part of the story" script, I decided to see if science had grabbed hold of the idea that trauma could yield long-term benefits. And then I found it—a whole field of research called *posttraumatic growth.*

Posttraumatic growth, also called *benefit finding*, is positive psychological change experienced as a result of adversity that leads to a higher level of functioning. In contrast to *resilience*, which is a more natural ability to bounce back, posttraumatic growth actually occurs in less resilient people who can't rise up without the hard work of changing their entire lives and worldviews. Resilience also emphasizes going "back to normal" after a trauma, whereas posttraumatic growth proposes people can actually *improve* as a result of it. Really?

Although I say this cautiously, tentatively, and sensitively, knowing how awful trauma is, yes, really.

Posttraumatic-growth research poses five areas of assessment that tend to predict outcomes:

1. *Appreciation of life.* People with a robust zest for life and a generally grateful attitude tend to grow from difficulty.
2. *Relationships with others.* People with warm, intimate human bonds both before and after the traumatic event tend to value those relationships more than ever.
3. *New possibilities in life.* People with an openness to change and a willingness to try new things tend to handle the life-altering nature of trauma with more adaptability.
4. *Personal strength.* People with self-efficacy, a sense that "I can survive," tend to power through tough experiences.
5. *Spiritual change.* People with a strong religious faith both before *and* after trauma tend to fare better after trauma.

All five of these traits are fruits of the gospel of Jesus Christ. Believers have the distinct advantage of a belief system for these traits. We can appreciate life because Jesus paid an infinite price for it. He made us to love and be loved, and our relationships are of the highest priority. We are focused on the future and have a reason we can accept loss gracefully, knowing it will be restored in the world to come. We have self-respect and self-control because God has declared us valuable and capable by His grace. And what of spiritual change? Well, I'll let Scripture answer that: "But we all, with unveiled face, beholding as in a mirror the glory of the Lord, are being transformed into the same image from glory to glory, just as by the Spirit of the Lord" (2 Corinthians 3:18).

For an assessment tool that will help you to see areas for improvement, go to "Posttraumatic Growth Survey" in the toolbox.

Case studies

Posttraumatic growth is more than the typical "setback is a setup for a comeback." Posttraumatic growth means the individual's life ultimately changes for the better, not *in spite* of trauma but *because* of trauma.

You heard me right.

Some researchers wanted to understand the causative factors behind *German angst,* which is a stereotype involving the German people's supposed pessimistic tendencies. First of all, the existence of a much higher level of angst among Germans didn't turn out to be true—the margin was small. But more important is what happened during the study. The researchers thought they would find a positive correlation between the cities most devastated by World War II bombings and the inhabitants' neuroticism levels.

They found the exact opposite: "Cities with more severe bombings show more resilience today (lower levels of neurotic traits and mental health problems in the face of a current major stressor—economic hardship)."[6]

The Dresden bombing killed up to twenty-five thousand people within a few days. Years later, researchers showed up, assuming to confirm that the terror had been passed down through the generations. Instead, they found "a positive correlation between PTG and traumatic exposure in addition to internal control beliefs."[7]

A more recent example involves a brain concussion that failed to heal properly. This injury caused game designer Jane McGonigal to spend a month in bed, wanting to die. In a moment of determination, she said, "I am either going to kill myself, or I'm going to turn this into a game." She knew games had the potential to bring out several positive traits: creativity, determination, optimism, and a willingness to ask for help. "I created a role-playing recovery game called Jane the Concussion Slayer." Jane called her identical twin sister, Kelly, and asked her to join in the game to help heal her brain. While the headaches and cognitive symptoms lingered, Jane reported, "Within just a couple days of starting to play, that fog of depression and anxiety went away. It just vanished." She renamed the game *SuperBetter* and began to market it to people with conditions such as cancer, Crohn's disease, and amyotrophic lateral sclerosis, receiving positive feedback from the participants. "Some people get stronger and happier after a traumatic event," she says. "That's what was happening to us."[8]

Jane points out that the top five regrets of dying people can be prevented by the top five aspects of posttraumatic growth.

Regrets of the dying	Posttraumatic growth traits
"I wish I hadn't worked so hard."	"My priorities have changed." "I'm not afraid to do what makes me happy."
"I wish I had stayed in touch with my friends."	"I feel closer to my friends and family."
"I wish I had let myself be happier."	"I understand myself better. I know who I really am now."
"I wish I'd had the courage to express my true self."	"I have a new sense of meaning and purpose in my life."
"I wish I'd lived a life true to my dreams, instead of what others expected of me."	"I'm better able to focus on my goals and dreams."

In a similar way, Kay Wilson, from our initial story, bears the permanent scars of her near-murder in the Jerusalem forest. She says,

Within thirty minutes, all I had ever known had been plundered and was lost forever. It was a personal *Horban Bayit*, a microcosm of the Destruction of the Temple.

My friend was destroyed.

My health was destroyed.

My ability to work was destroyed and so was the dignity that comes [from] providing for myself.

My independence was destroyed.

My income was destroyed.

My appetite was destroyed.

My pain-free existence was destroyed.

My sleep was destroyed.

My routine was destroyed.

My solace of being alone was destroyed.

My luxury of engaging in the mundane was destroyed.

My hope of ever being truly understood by another was destroyed.

My anonymity was destroyed.

My humanity was destroyed.

My innocence was destroyed.

My sense of security was destroyed.

My reputation was destroyed.

The knife tore through my flesh and shredded all that I had—everything, that is, except for "me.". . .

I believe with an imperfect faith that the question is not "why" did this happen to me, but rather "how" can I incorporate this grisly event into the rhythm of my life in a manner that guards me from becoming like those who tried to murder me.

I believe with an imperfect faith in a G-d of justice who has promised that vengeance is His.[9]

Kay travels the world speaking to global audiences, hoping to "dispel hatred, whether toward Arabs or Jews."[10] She says,

I choose to listen out for the songs of the birds and not just hear the whimper of my friend. And I choose to smell those beautiful, fragrant Jerusalem pines and not just smell the vomit behind my gag. And it's those step-by-step momentary choices that have enabled me, a survivor of Arab terrorism, to reach out to an Arab teenager who was undergoing death threats from members of his own community and at the risk of my own life hide him in my house. It has enabled me, a survivor of Islamist terrorism, to travel in Egypt and hang out with a wonderful Muslim friend. And it has enabled me, a survivor of Palestinian terrorism, to reach out to a Palestinian friend and via social media, help him find people, human resources, to aid him to kickstart a small business. Because like me, my Palestinian friend knows that to be shackled in individual or collective victimhood is not helpful, kind, true, or moral.[11]

That's what I call PTG. Could we who believe in the Redeemer likewise allow Him to buy back our traumas for good?

DISCUSSION QUESTIONS

1. Share something in your life that would qualify as a trauma.

2. Did people validate the trauma? Who were these people, and how did they validate it?

3. What do you think keeps people from validating trauma survivors?

4. Does it surprise you that many of the weight-loss clinic dropouts had been sexually abused? Why, or why not?

5. Does it discourage you or encourage you to see the ACE study? Why?

6. What feelings do you experience in knowing that Jesus can redeem your traumas for good?

7. Which of the five areas of growth after trauma do you relate to? Can you give examples?

8. Specifically, did your traumatic experiences change your relationships? How?

9. Have your traumas changed your purpose in life? How?

10. Why do some traumatized people become more positive and optimistic?

---

1. Wikipedia, s.v. "Murders of Neta Sorek and Kristine Luken," last updated April 21, 2019, https://en.wikipedia.org/wiki/Murders_of_Neta_Sorek_and_Kristine_Luken.

2. Lawrence Calhoun, email correspondence with author, July 12, 2018.

3. American Psychiatric Association, *Diagnostic and Statistical Manual of Mental Disorders*, 5th ed. (Arlington, VA: American Psychiatric Association, 2013), 271.

4. American Psychiatric Association, *Diagnostic and Statistical Manual*, 272.

5. Jane Ellen Stevens, "Toxic Stress From Childhood Trauma Causes Obesity, Too," ACES Too High News, May 23, 2012, https://acestoohigh.com/2012/05/23/toxic-stress-from-childhood-trauma-causes-obesity-too/.

6. Martin Obschonka et al., "Did Strategic Bombing in the Second World War Lead to 'German Angst'? A Large-Scale Empirical Test Across 89 German Cities," in "Personality and Social Structure," special issue, *European Journal of Personality* 31, no. 3 (May/June 2017): 234–257, https://doi.org/10.1002/per.2104.

7. Rita Rosner and Steve Powell, "Posttraumatic Growth After War," in *Handbook of Posttraumatic Growth: Research and Practice,* ed. Richard G. Tedeschi and Lawrence G. Calhoun (New York: Psychology Press, 2014), 202.

8. Jane McGonigal, "The Game That Can Give You 10 Extra Years of Life," TEDGlobal 2012, June 2012, video, 19:24, https://www.ted.com/talks/jane_mcgonigal_the_game_that_can_give_you_10_extra_years_of_life?language=en.

9. Kay Wilson, "I Believe With an Imperfect Faith," *The Blogs* (blog), *Times of Israel*, December 23, 2014, https://blogs .timesofisrael.com/i-believe-with-an-imperfect-faith/.

10. Lorna Collier, "Growth After Trauma: Why Are Some People More Resilient Than Others—and Can It Be Taught?" *Monitor on Psychology* 47, no. 10 (November 2016): 48, https://www.apa.org/monitor/2016/11/growth-trauma.

11. Kay Wilson, "Step by Step: The Idiot's Guide to Surviving a Machete Attack," June 9, 2015, Tedx Talks video, 16:01, https://www.youtube.com/watch?v=GMUkNWv-0nU.

Crazy Compassion

My friend Nicole appears to be a typical housewife, but it's only an appearance. Look closer, and you see a crazy woman.

Nicole's grandfather raped her repeatedly when she was just a small child. During her remaining childhood and teen years, she tried to avoid the trauma, only to have it leak out in extreme anxiety: Wearing blue jeans to bed every night to fend off rapists. Steering her cart away from grocery-store aisles where men stood. Avoiding open spaces that exposed her back. Walking off sidewalks when men walked toward her. Panic attacks when unfamiliar men walked behind her. Cringing when a man picked up and held a little girl.

Finally, Nicole broke her story as a young adult. It was posted on an online forum, which disseminated it around the world, effectively turning her into a blazing fire toward which a horde of cold and weary abuse survivors flocked to warm themselves and tell their stories. An average day in the life of Nicole finds her mothering her four kids, but this is interspersed with phone calls from those survivors. Imagine a housewife in jeans, T-shirt, no makeup, brown hair sticking to her forehead from the steam of lunch cooking on the stove, with a cell phone wedged between her cheek and shoulder, shouting to her boys in the backyard, "Do *not* eat that," and then speaking into the phone, "OK, when did the rape occur? Let me get my laptop." She says, "It's a demanding balancing act, trying to help all the people who contact me, without cheating my family out of time. But I believe God gives wisdom and strength in answer to prayer, for the tasks He asks us to do. And when I get weary, I always try to keep in mind where I might have been if no one had taken the time to help me."[1]

Sympathy is the feeling of pity and sorrow for others' misfortune. Sympathy comes from a place of goodwill, but it remains at a distance from the other. Because of that distance, it can become selfish, as in focusing on *my* suffering in response to your suffering, rather than your suffering. In sympathy, the sense of autonomy stays put. Sympathy can blossom into empathy and compassion, or it can morph into apathy.

Empathy takes a step closer to the other person by vicariously experiencing his or her feelings. In empathy, I am not simply feeling bad *for* you, I am feeling your bad *with* you. Empathy dismantles my self-concern and joins me to you, relieving you of the isolating effects of your pain. Once I feel empathy for you, I am faced with a choice as to whether to take the next step of doing something about your plight.

Compassion takes action on sympathy and empathy.* Compassion beats a path from the heart to the volitional center of the head and chooses to do something about the plight of one's object of empathy. Compassion actualizes and channels the energy of intense emotions, funneling it into tangible, measurable help.

Building on empathy

Empathy is a powerful force in politics and commerce. Former president Barack Obama said the empathy deficit in the United States was a more serious problem than the budget deficit.[2] His perceived greater empathy may have won him the 2012 presidential election over Mitt Romney, while Hillary Clinton's cold, aloof public image may have cost her the election in 2016. Emotive, empathic brands sell more products. In 2017, Delta treated delayed passengers to a pizza party and spread videos of it all over the internet. Dove's "Real Beauty Sketches" marketing campaign empathized with women's insecurities about their appearance. Amazon.com searches yield more than fifteen hundred books with the word *empathy* in their titles.

Empathy means big money these days.

But simple emotional empathy may not be all that we need to make a difference in the world. Apparently, even *rats* can experience empathy. A 2011 University of Chicago study showed that a rat would release another rat from a cage without being given a reward. The rats learned to open a restrainer to release other caged rats even when they didn't get to

---

* My intention in distinguishing between these traits is not to dogmatize the use of certain words. Language is best left flexible, with word use adapting to the context.

play with those rats. More amazing still, when presented with two cages, one containing another rat and the other containing chocolate, they chose to open *both* cages and share the chocolate.[3]

Is empathy the king of emotions if *rats* can experience it? After all, if the mirror neurons that mediate emotional empathy provide a sense of pleasure when another person experiences pleasure, couldn't we want others to experience pleasure for purely selfish reasons? Sorry if I am raining on the empathy parade, but stay with me while I round this out.

Limits of emotional empathy

In-group bias. Because we more easily relate to people like us, we will naturally tend to limit our circle of concern to our own kind of person—racial, religious, ideological, ethnic, and so on. For example, one study revealed that when shown a needle penetrating a hand, both black and white participants experienced more empathy for people of their own color. Intriguingly, this appeared to occur more as a function of culturally acquired racial prejudice rather than the target simply being different: the researchers targeted a violet hand and got an empathic response similar to a same-race response.[4]

Racial bias at its worst can literally turn off the faucet of emotional empathy, leading us to see certain groups as subhuman! Only 162 years ago, the US Supreme Court ruled against the black slave Dred Scott when he appealed to the court for his freedom. Chief Justice Roger B. Taney said that blacks could never become citizens, that the Declaration of Independence's statement that "all men are created equal" didn't apply to blacks because they weren't *men*, and that black people could be "bought and sold and treated as an ordinary article of merchandise and traffic, whenever profit could be made."[5]

Self-referencing. Empathy is an emotional resonance with others mediated by mirror neurons that have the unique ability to connect one nervous system with another. Because of our natural bent toward self-centeredness, even empathy can become self-referenced. I may feel awkward in response to observing a socially awkward person, but then I will become more concerned with alleviating my own feelings of vicarious embarrassment than with alleviating the individual's feelings of awkwardness. This can lead to avoidance of needy people.

Compassion fatigue. This well-known phenomenon affects people in helping professions and can lead to extreme burnout. Among other important preventatives, emotional boundary setting becomes essential to helpers. Empathy appears to come in a limited, exhaustible supply that we must respect, constantly recharging at the feet of Jesus.

Manipulation of empathy. While many believe sociopaths and psychopaths lack empathy, they may actually possess just as strong an empathy as normal people but be more adroit in turning it off. In a study led by the author of *The Empathic Brain*, Christian Keysers, researchers showed a group of twenty-one criminal psychopaths movies of people inflicting harm on one another. Predictably, scans revealed the activation of the empathy regions of the brains of the participants as below average. Keysers remembers chatting with one of the most severe psychopaths and finding him very pleasant. He remarked on how normal the man seemed. The researchers then decided to have the participants watch the movies again, this time instructing them to feel empathy. Their empathy activation came up to normal levels.[6]

Some people believe the kind of empathy sociopaths and psychopaths possess is only the cognitive variety. Whether this is true or not, sociopaths and psychopaths know how to manipulate others' emotional empathy to the max. The fatal attraction between an empath and a narcissist is the stuff of legends, with the empath believing, forgiving, and trusting, and the narcissist manipulating to the full. A pathologically selfish person sees another individual in very instrumental terms, as "an obstacle in the way of his own advancement, or a steppingstone on which he himself may climb to a higher place."[7]

The pitfalls of emotional empathy don't merit its rejection, though. Rather, we should cultivate it, discipline it, and build on it. Enter a phenomenon called *cognitive empathy.* Psychologists note a distinction between emotional empathy, which is based on feeling, and cognitive empathy, which is based on an intellectual understanding of how others think and feel. This balancing of empathy can make a huge difference in what actions we take in response to suffering.

Finally, compassion is the flowing of empathy, both emotional and cognitive, into positive, altruistic, and appropriate action. Empathy experts Tania Singer and Olga Klimecki point out that, in contrast to passive emotional empathy, "compassionate responses are based on positive, other-oriented feelings and the activation of prosocial motivation and behavior."[8] In other words, in terms of motivating selfless sacrifice for others, compassion crowns empathy with true dignity and virtue.

God's empathy, God's compassion

Let's shift our focus to what God's Word says about empathy and compassion. Certainly, God wants us to feel with others and "rejoice with those who rejoice, and weep with those who weep" (Romans 12:15). We are told, "Carry each other's burdens, and in this way you will fulfill the law of Christ" (Galatians 6:2, NIV). An awareness that another person truly feels our pain and carries our stories in his or her heart can lift a heavy burden. The process is complete when compassion steps in at the right time, intervening to protect and provide.

Clearly, God's heart overflows with empathy. He hears us:

- "Hear, O LORD, when I cry with my voice!" (Psalm 27:7).
- "The righteous cry out, and the LORD hears" (Psalm 34:17).
- "I will cry to You, when my heart is overwhelmed" (Psalm 61:2).

Hearing involves taking in what another is putting out—even raw, painful emotions. Empathic or active listening, which utilizes the principle that "everyone should be quick to listen, slow to speak and slow to become angry," can provide the basis for conflict resolution (James 1:19, NIV). In counseling sessions, I often coach struggling couples in empathy-based listening and watch them work out long-standing conflict within a short period. Why? Because empathy warms the substance of a relationship, softening hard edges and making it possible to mold the relationship into a better shape.

God's deep empathy for humanity speaks the loudest in Jesus. The act of becoming a member of the fallen race demonstrated, among other things, that love compelled Him to share our human experience. "For this reason he had to be made like them, fully human in every way, in order that he might become a merciful and faithful high priest in service to God, and that he might make atonement for the sins of the people. Because he himself suffered when he was tempted, he is able to help those who are being tempted" (Hebrews 2:17, 18, NIV). Jesus' emotional investment in the human race shines in the Incarnation. "For we do not have a high priest who is unable to empathize with our

For help using empathic listening skills, see "Establishing Empathy With EAR" in the toolbox. For a conflict resolution technique using empathic listening, see "The Floor Technique" in the toolbox.

weaknesses, but we have one who has been tempted in every way, just as we are—yet he did not sin" (Hebrews 4:15, NIV). Put positively, we *do* have an empathic High Priest. Alleluia!

An element of thoughtfulness, an informed intentionality, is visible in God's compassion toward humanity. He says, "I will have compassion on whom I will have compassion" (Exodus 33:19). "For the LORD will judge His people and have compassion on His servants" (Deuteronomy 32:36). Notice that judging and compassion are in the same package! God judges, or discerns, our need for compassion through careful consideration of our situation. Like a good earthly father, God chastens those He loves, disciplining us for our good, even as our tears tug at His heart (see Hebrews 12:6). Were God to practice pure emotional empathy, He would fail as a parent, as many parents do today. But He acts upon His tender feelings toward us with strategic actions designed to relieve our suffering.

More of God's compassion

The Bible is full of other examples of compassion:

- "Can a woman forget her nursing child, and not have compassion on the son of her womb? Surely they may forget, yet I will not forget you" (Isaiah 49:15).
- "Then it shall be, after I have plucked them out, that I will return and have compassion on them and bring them back, everyone to his heritage and everyone to his land" (Jeremiah 12:15).
- "Through the LORD's mercies we are not consumed, because His compassions fail not" (Lamentations 3:22).
- "But when He [Jesus] saw the multitudes, He was moved with compassion for them, because they were weary and scattered, like sheep having no shepherd" (Matthew 9:36).
- "Then Jesus, moved with compassion, stretched out His hand and touched [the leper] . . . and said to him, 'I am willing; be cleansed' " (Mark 1:41).
- "And on some have compassion, making a distinction; but others save with fear, pulling them out of the fire, hating even the garment defiled by the flesh" (Jude 22, 23).

After trauma

Compassion brings the elements of emotional and cognitive empathy to bear on the choice to live a life that channels God's love. But how do we become compassionate?

The answer may surprise you. The most reliable route to compassion is through our own journey of suffering. What I am proposing is that the painful experiences we have cataloged—the abuse we have suffered, the random disasters we have endured, and the uphill battles that bring us to tears—those things can potentially make us experts in compassion. Of course, there's no guarantee. The trajectory of trauma can be devastating, transformative, or most often, some of both. The harsh reality of a horrible experience shatters the inner world of the victim. But in the reconstruction process, God can transform the raw nerve of trauma into a mighty instrument of help for other trauma survivors. Trauma creates a neurological and emotional basis for a life of compassion.

Samantha Nelson's pastor seemed like a kind man with a heart to help her cope with an experience that had triggered the pain and memories of her past abuse—until he raped her in the office where he was supposed to be counseling her. Of course, she went from bad to worse, ultimately despairing of life itself, keeping the secret from her husband, Steve, until he discovered what the pastor had been doing to her and confronted Samantha and the pastor about it. Through a long, arduous process of healing and education, she came through with a determined purpose to provide the very lifeline she didn't have as a survivor of sexual abuse by clergy. Samantha and Steve founded the Hope of Survivors ministry (THOS), which, for the past two decades, has served victims of clergy sexual abuse in all fifty states and in thirty-nine countries. THOS is registered as a nonprofit organization in the United States, Australia, and Romania, with divisions in Canada, the United Kingdom, the Philippines, Trinidad and Tobago, and South Africa. On average, there are ten thousand to fifteen thousand unique visitors to their website per month, with two new victims per week contacting them for help.

Some shun the idea of trauma survivors helping others survive trauma. "You will get too triggered. You won't be able to be objective. You will burn out," they say. And they have a point. In counseling, we call these types of responses *vicarious trauma*, or *secondary trauma*. Experts understand that such experiences can harm therapists and even render them less effective.[9] But they can also make them *more* effective.

Our own personal trauma gives us a neurological and experiential basis for understanding the trauma of others. What makes us more "trauma informed"—sensitive to and knowledgeable about trauma—than to have experienced it? Personal-experience-fueled empathy *alone* can be a sufficient reason for the traumatized to become great helpers, but there's more. Our battle scars make us more trustworthy to the wounded. Sharing our own stories of recovery can not only increase our credibility with hurting people but also kindle hope that they, too, can come out the other side and become helpers. Trauma survivors who pass through their own journey of healing, continually realizing their need for divine and human support and good, solid self-care practices, can be wonderfully effective in helping other trauma survivors. In fact, God would have us create a process of helping by sharing what we've learned from others, who in turn pass their new knowledge onto others, until everyone is eventually helped. That process will continue until Jesus comes again and even beyond into the thousand-year therapy session called the millennium, after which "God will wipe away every tear from their eyes" (Revelation 21:4).

Back to Nicole

Nicole says,

I used to believe I could never become a wife or mother, because I was so terrified of physical intimacy, and I could hardly bear to even watch a man pick up a little girl. But now that I've gone through the process of healing, I love being a wife and mother. I'm able to let my kids go places and do things without being hyper-vigilant. I balance my time between homeschooling, cooking wholesome meals and keeping up with the house, and squeeze in time to counsel and answer emails when I can. I try to make sure I direct as many of the people who contact me as possible to some source of healing, whether a book or a fellow counselor. And of course, Jesus, the Wonderful Counselor.

People who don't want to delve into the complex and slow-moving process of helping people heal from sexual trauma rejoice to hear stories like mine. They point to my life and say, "See, sexual abuse survivors don't have to wrap their identities around the past abuse! They can live rich and fulfilling lives that are unstained by what happened a long time ago."

They are right, to a point. But actually, Nicole has been unalterably changed by her trauma. It drives her to help victims, dig down into the muck and mire of abuse situations, and engage in a messy process in which it is impossible not to make mistakes. She is like a woman on fire. She can't stop trying to end abuse any more than she can stop breathing. In short, she is crazy—crazy compassionate.

Crazy compassionate people believe that God "comforts us in all our tribulation, that we may be able to comfort those who are in any trouble, with the comfort with which we ourselves are comforted by God. . . . If we are afflicted, it is for your consolation and salvation" (2 Corinthians 1:4, 6). Our trauma seems futile, a crippling of our energies and well-being, until we see God transform it into an avenue of grace to others.

DISCUSSION QUESTIONS

1. Share a time when you received empathy from another person.

2. How does it feel to be on the receiving end of empathy? On the giving end?

3. Compassion has been defined as empathy in action. When have you seen genuine compassion?

4. We are told to weep with those who weep. What purpose does this serve?

5. Share a time when empathy contributed to conflict resolution.

6. One of the most reliable routes to compassion is our own suffering. How does this fact change your view of suffering?

7. How does trauma affect a person's ability to help other victims of trauma?

8. Share a time when you experienced secondary trauma, when people who could have offered empathy and support did not.

9. The enemy wrote the first chapter of the book titled *I Hate You*. God's Word corrects this lie with the truth that we are loved with an everlasting love. How will this truth change the way you live?

10. Share one way you can follow in the footsteps of Jesus and extend compassion to suffering people around you.

1. Personal text exchange between author and "Nicole."

2. Mark Honigsbaum, "Barack Obama and the 'Empathy Deficit,' " *Guardian*, January 4, 2013, https://www.theguardian.com/science/2013/jan/04/barack-obama-empathy-deficit.

3. Inbal Ben-Ami Bartal, Jean Decety, and Peggy Mason, "Empathy and Pro-Social Behavior in Rats," *Science* 334, no. 6061 (December 2011): 1427–1430, http://www.jstor.org/stable/41352251.

4. Joan Y. Chiao and Vani A. Mathur, "Intergroup Empathy: How Does Race Affect Empathic Neural Responses?" *Current Biology* 20, no. 11 (June 2010): 478–480, https://www.cell.com/action/showPdf?pii=S0960-9822(10)00430-6.

5. "Dred Scott Case: The Supreme Court Decision," *Africans in America*, PBS, accessed June 11, 2019, https://www.pbs.org/wgbh/aia/part4/4h2933t.html.

6. Christian Keysers, "Inside the Mind of a Psychopath—Empathic, but Not Always," *Psychology Today,* July 24, 2013, https://www.psychologytoday.com/us/blog/the-empathic-brain/201307/inside-the-mind-psychopath-empathic-not-always.

7. Ellen G. White, *The Desire of Ages* (Mountain View, CA: Pacific Press®, 1940), 436.

8. Tania Singer and Olga Klimecki, "Empathy and Compassion," *Current Biology* 24, no. 18 (September, 22, 2014): 875–878, https://www.cell.com/action/showPdf?pii=S0960-9822(14)00770-2.

9. Leo Sexton, "Vicarious Traumatisation of Counsellors and Effects on Their Workplaces," *British Journal of Guidance and Counselling* 27, no. 3 (1999): 393–403, https://doi.org/10.1080/03069889908256279.

Loneliness Kissed Love

I have a confession to make. While reading a research piece for this chapter, a review that surveyed a large number of scientific papers on social dynamics brought me to tears. People don't typically cry while reading scientific papers that say things like "activation of the HPA axis involves a cascade of signals that results in release of ACTH from the pituitary and cortisol from the adrenal cortex."[1] But I did. Why? Because in the scientific data, I saw the signature of God—the truth that He created us for love.

In fact, science arrives at the same conclusion that all other disciplines do. Through the language of science, we hear the same heartbeat that pulsates in more expressive tones through literature, music, and the arts. Whether you are a writer of books and poetry, a troubadour plucking guitar strings, a painter with a palette and an easel, or a lab-coated scientist, your discipline leads you to the conclusion to which all other disciplines eventually lead: people are made to love and be loved.

An ancillary truth is that people are lonely, and loneliness hurts.

Webster's dictionary defines *loneliness* as "being without company" and "cut off from others."[2] Social scientists define it as a "distressing feeling that accompanies the perception that one's social needs are not being met by the quantity or especially the quality of one's social relationships."[3] Loneliness is the social equivalent of physical pain, hunger, and thirst. It's not necessarily being physically alone as much as being emotionally alone and bearing the chilling sense of insignificance that comes with heart isolation.

Stephanie Cacioppo is positioned as perhaps no other social scientist to speak to these issues. For one, she can speak as a scientist whose life work has been to understand the science of human bonding. Second, she can speak as someone whose research partner, John

Cacioppo, was an expert on loneliness. Finally, she can speak as a human whose life experience uncannily turned out to be a case study in loneliness and love.

Stephanie Ortigue lived in Geneva, Switzerland, and John Cacioppo lived in Chicago, Illinois, United States, when they met in Shanghai at a conference for the Society for Social Neuroscience, which John had helped found. By chance, they sat next to each other at the official dinner at the close of the conference, finding themselves engrossed in conversation and their mutual attraction. They married within a year. Stephanie took John's surname and became Stephanie Cacioppo. She says, "When we got married I had more than 50 publications under my maiden name, so when I changed it my colleagues kept saying, what are you doing? . . . But I didn't mind. For me the love is more important than having a big ego about my name and publications."[4]

The University of Chicago, where John directed the Center for Cognitive and Social Neuroscience, hired Stephanie to run its electrical neuroimaging lab, and the two settled in.[5] We might say that in the union of the Cacioppos, loneliness kissed love.

Prevalence and effects

John Cacioppo's research tells us that loneliness is pandemic and appears to be on the rise. In the United States, it increased from 20 percent in the 1980s to 40 percent in 2013.[6] A full 80 percent of those under eighteen and 40 percent of those over sixty-five report being lonely. Fortunately, the levels of loneliness dip somewhat through the middle-adult years when life is at its busiest and many people have children at home.[7] But the overall rise in loneliness should trouble us.

Loneliness has a huge impact on health. It has been associated with cardiovascular health problems, elevated blood pressure, and numerous other health issues. The low-level anxiety often experienced by lonely people afflicts their sleep as well; the lonely tend to have less restorative sleep due to more frequent nightly microawakenings.[8] As if all this wasn't already depressing enough, let me throw in one more statistic: loneliness increases the mortality rate by 26 percent.[9]

Loneliness risks
- Cardiovascular disease
- Elevated blood pressure

- Cognitive decline
- Alzheimer's disease
- Poor emotion regulation
- Less physical exercise
- Personality disorders
- Psychosis
- Suicide
- Diminished executive control
- Poor sleep

We thrive best in a community. British anthropologist Robin Dunbar studied the brains of primates and found a correlation between a primate's neocortex size and its social-group size: the larger the neocortex, the larger the social group. Based on his findings, he calculated that human beings are capable of 150 social connections, defined as a knowledge of another person and how he or she connects to the social group.[10]

Beyond the wider sphere of association, the quality of the narrower sphere of close connections comes into play in social well-being. The famous Blue Zones study discovered that some of the longest-living people in the world come from a small Japanese island called Okinawa. Okinawans have five to six good friends—people on whom they can depend in times of need. In referring to the health-giving power of good friends, Blue Zones study author Dan Buettner points out that friendships in our day-to-day lives add years to life and life to those years.[11] But those friendships are becoming a rarity. The global health company Cigna did a survey of twenty thousand Americans and found the following shocking trends: three in four Americans feel that no one understands them; two in five feel their relationships aren't meaningful; "only around half of Americans (53%) have meaningful in-person social interactions."[12]

What causes loneliness?

It can't be overemphasized that God designed us for connection with others. We see throughout human development that God organized life in such a way that every stage builds the brain for love. It begins with the primary caregiver of the infant, typically the mother. The mother engages in a multiplicity of bonding behaviors with the baby. For instance, she may feed the baby from her own body, a process that floods both bodies with bonding chemicals and allows for direct gazing into each other's eyes. If all goes well with the mother-child bonding, this bond creates the neurological capacity for future bonds with the dad, siblings, friends, and mate. Each stage builds on the last and prepares for the next.

Brain development flourishes when family bonds are strong. But when deprived of secure bonds, a child comes into adulthood with a poorly conditioned emotional brain. The most severe cases develop *reactive attachment disorder*, but an insecurely attached child will also be susceptible to other disorders, such as anxiety and depression. Babies essentially have two states—securely attached or insecurely attached—and their health and happiness sync fully to secure attachment. A lack of touch-based bonding in orphanages has led to a high incidence of a condition called *nonorganic failure to thrive*, which can lead to developmental problems and even death. The relational fragility of a baby is an apt metaphor for human life beyond infancy. When securely bonded, we thrive; when lonely, we fail to thrive.

Too often, we numb the pain of loneliness through escapist behaviors, such as drugs, alcohol, sex, materialism, video games, pornography, and other distractions. Once these distractions take on a life of their own, they develop into addictions. Addiction compromises the relationship-building, pro-social part of the brain, driving us further into the loneliness that led us to the addiction in the first place. As with addiction, loneliness both precedes and follows mental disorders, such as anxiety, depression, and psychotic and personality disorders.

Many people express concerns about the effect of social media on loneliness. As it turns out, it can have a positive or negative effect, depending on how we use it. Social media "snacking"—browsing others' profiles and threads without engaging—can be problematic.

If you think you may have a problem with social media, check out the "Social Media Disorder Scale" in the toolbox.

Another troublesome approach is the practice of comparison: when you compare the pretty *outside* of someone's life to the ugly *inside* of yours. But like other forms of media, social media's danger lies mostly in what it displaces, chiefly face-to-face conversation free of distractions. One study found that college seniors with high numbers of Facebook friends were better adjusted socially; for college freshman, the correlation was reversed. The researchers ultimately discovered that the seniors were using Facebook to communicate with friends at college, while the freshman were using it to connect with friends from high school, meaning that they weren't getting out and making new friends![13] When social media facilitates a real social life, it can fight loneliness, but when it displaces a real social life, it has the opposite effect.

Not to add moral shame to an already painful situation, but selfishness can correlate with loneliness.[14] The connection makes sense: loneliness arouses the limbic system, putting us in survival mode, which is a state where we fend for ourselves. Rather than trusting others to look out for our interests, those of us who are isolative individuals feel we must look out for our own, increasing our isolation.

The selfishness-curbing effect of a relationship is part of why God calls the church to become an others-centered community actuated by principles of altruism. "Let each of you look out not only for his own interests, but also for the interests of others" (Philippians 2:4). Trusting and believing that other people care about us loosens the grip of selfishness on our hearts.

One of the most basic contributors to loneliness is our core-belief system regarding love. Core beliefs form the substrata of our automatic thoughts, feeding them constantly with big-picture assumptions. Core beliefs form in the limbic, nonverbal part of the brain, often as a result of our incorrect interpretation of our life experiences. Core beliefs organize themselves into a *schema*, which is a network of beliefs through which we continue to interpret our life experiences. Our schemata drive our attention—people are more likely to notice things that fit into their schemata—and our interpretation of events. Once we establish core narratives, we tend to interpret new experiences to fit the narrative, rather than letting new experiences expand the narrative.

For help in identifying your core beliefs, see "Finding and Replacing Core Lies" in the toolbox. For help with forming relationships, see "Making Friends, Keeping Friends" in the toolbox.

The gospel enters

This is the point where the gospel powerfully redirects the loneliness trajectory. Through the gospel, we become willing to adopt a new narrative—one based on powerful positives about love and relationships rather than the gloomy core beliefs that drove us before.

While the Bible does say that death is our primary fear, I would like to make a case for fear of social death as our core fear (Hebrews 2:15). Recall that the disciple Peter, unafraid to face physical death, drew his sword in front of a cohort of fully armed Roman soldiers. Yet only a few hours later, Peter crumbled before the social death of ridicule in the temple courtyard, leading him to deny Jesus with cursing and swearing. His physical death in the Garden would have been accompanied by human praise of his heroism, making it seem less threatening than the social shaming he received from the Sanhedrin servants.

Jesus' physical death was hastened by His social death. The crushing sense of being cut off from His Father overwhelmed His nervous system. He cried, "Why have You forsaken Me?" because His Father's face disappeared as the Son bore the sins of the world (Matthew 27:46). "He was despised, and we did not esteem Him" (Isaiah 53:3).

The gospel says that Jesus took our place, bearing our utter aloneness, so that we could have access to all the riches of eternal love in both the divine and human realms. Faith lays hold of these truths, creating a channel whereby God's love can pour into our souls. Allowing the Holy Spirit to transform our core beliefs puts us in the middle of an entirely new narrative and, at the same time, gives us a new lens through which to interpret life.

Loneliness is part of the story—but not all of the story.

As believers, we will continue to experience loneliness. The gospel doesn't remove our humanity; it gives us the power to live it fully. "Turn Yourself to me, and have mercy on me," said the psalmist, "for I am desolate and afflicted" (Psalm 25:16). But rather than a soul-numbing dead end, loneliness becomes a passageway into deeper fellowship with God and, ultimately, with our brothers and sisters. God deepens us to make us more capable of profound love. Knowing the infinite riches of God's love held in store for us, we are safe to enter the human realm with all of its perils and pain.

Breaking the loneliness cycle

Lonely people often find themselves in a self-perpetuating succession of events that begins with loneliness and ends with more loneliness. The succession looks something like this: People feel lonely. They adopt a mind-set of social poverty—"No one loves me." Their emptiness and neediness make them vulnerable, which they find shameful and embarrassing. As a result, they increase their avoidance of true intimacy, ending up exactly where they started—lonely.

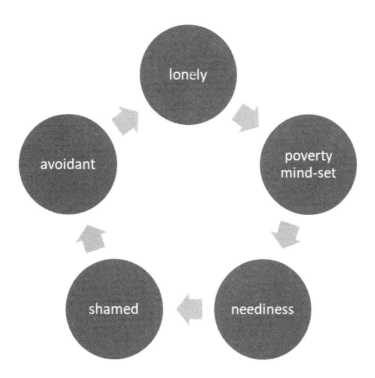

Where can this sickening cycle of despair be broken? I believe God breaks in at the point of the poverty mind-set. We come to human relationships with a deficiency so profound that no human can fill it. But at the moment faith embraces the truth that God really does love us personally, deeply, intimately, and fully, we can transition from a poverty mind-set to one of abundance.

It's not quite that we don't need human relationships, because God has designed us to connect both vertically and horizontally; but it's that if we go to human relationships to fill our basic existential cup, we set ourselves up for relational disappointment. In contrast, we go to human relationships to join in the celebration of a wealth of love flowing from God's heart to all of His blessed children, to share what God has already given us, and to receive the same from His other children. "God sets the solitary in families" (Psalm 68:6, NIV).

"Hope does not disappoint, because the love of God has been poured out in our hearts by the Holy Spirit who was given to us" (Romans 5:5). The core belief that we are unloved, a belief that leaves lonely people locked in a cycle of pain, is *fundamentally untrue.* The only thing that stands in the way of you walking confidently as a loved person in this world is your unbelief. Take heart, though; unbelief can be overcome through the simple choice to believe what God says.

It's simple. Do it. Believe you are loved. Then share from your abundance.

The following story illustrates the power of believing in love: Several decades ago, before the internet existed, a con artist named Don Lowry came up with a scheme to exploit the loneliness of single men. He created a catalog full of stock photos of beautiful models that he mailed out to a list of men. When the men opened the catalog, they found the pages full of attractive women offering to be pen pals—for a fee. Each woman went by the nickname "Angel." There was Angel Pamela, Angel Linda, Angel Kristina, and so on.

Many men jumped at the offer. They wrote to their "angels," and Don Lowry wrote back. After a while, the "angel" would ask for financial favors, and most men happily complied.

Between 1982 and 1985, more than thirty thousand men in the United States, Canada, and Mexico donated more than 4.5 million dollars. Don's greed finally got the best of him when "Angel Susan," one of his employees, wrecked a car while on drugs. Don tapped his network of lonely men, sending out photos of her injuries and soliciting money for the fallen angel's medical expenses. However, he kept the money for himself instead of giving it to Angel Susan, who flew to the police and turned Don in.

The funny part of this story is that several of the lonely men Don conned showed up at the trial and testified on his behalf, claiming that he had improved their lonely lives.[15] This proves that at least some of the bonding process is contingent upon our faith that someone loves us. Don's victims believed—albeit wrongly—that their "angels" really loved them, and this helped them to feel better. On the other extreme, we have solid, substantial evidence that the infinite God of heaven, our Creator, Redeemer, and Friend, loves us with an unfathomable, unsearchable, infinite love, and we fail to accept that comfort. Sometimes we do a worse job of believing the truth than Don's marks did of believing a lie!

Reframing loneliness

We can confidently reframe loneliness as more than just a negative feeling and experience, or worse yet, as an indication that we are fundamentally unlovable. Science and inspiration show that we actually need loneliness to motivate us into a more advantageous social position. Like physical pain tells the body it has a health problem, loneliness tells the heart it has a social problem. John Cacioppo says, "When I first started studying loneliness about 20 years ago, it was viewed as [an] affliction with no redeeming features." Through research, he came to believe that "loneliness is an aversive state that serves as a signal to attend to and take care of the social connections that define us as a species."[16]

> *For a simple guide to the practical aspects of building relationships, refer back to "Making Friends, Keeping Friends" in the toolbox. For help with working through the forgiveness process for past relationship wounds, see "Forgiveness" in the toolbox.*

Stephanie Cacioppo concurs: "Loneliness, which compels us to bond with others, gives us what we call Humanity."[17]

Tragically, John Cacioppo unexpectedly died only seven years into his marriage to Stephanie. She says, "I did not know what true love was until I met my husband. John taught me what true love really means. And now, thanks to my husband, I am on the verge of knowing what true eternal love is."[18]

DISCUSSION QUESTIONS

1. Share a time in your life when you experienced loneliness.

2. How do you feel when you see that other people are lonely?

3. Loneliness can cause or contribute to health problems. What is one big benefit of loneliness?

4. As you think about human life, what are some evidences that God created love for us?

5. Addiction can be an effort to numb the pain of loneliness. Share a time when you have experienced this.

6. How can people use social media to their benefit?

7. How does God break into the cycle of loneliness, shame, and avoidance?

8. Do we come to human relationships with an empty cup, a cup full of God's love, or both?

9. The core belief that we are unloved is fundamentally untrue. How does it feel to realize this?

10. Name a practical way you can celebrate the love of God in fellowship with other people.

1. Louise C. Hawkley and John T. Cacioppo, "Loneliness Matters: A Theoretical and Empirical Review of Consequences and Mechanisms," *Annals of Behavioral Medicine* 40, no. 2 (October 2010): 218–227, https://www.ncbi.nlm.nih.gov/pmc/articles/PMC3874845/.

2. *Webster's Third New International Dictionary*, Unabridged ed., s.v. "lonely," accessed June 12, 2019, http://unabridged.merriam-webster.com.

3. Hawkley and Cacioppo, "Loneliness Matters."

4. Katie Worth, "When Scientists Are Mad About Each Other," *Scientific American*, February 14, 2014, https://www.scientificamerican.com/article/when-scientists-are-mad-about-each-other/.

5. Christopher Weber, "Psychology's John and Stephanie Cacioppo: Love on the Brain," Division of the Social Sciences, University of Chicago, October 25, 2015, https://socialsciences.uchicago.edu/story/psychologys-john-and-stephanie-cacioppo-love-brain.

6. Jessica Olien, "Loneliness Is Deadly," Medical Examiner, *Slate*, August 23, 2013, https://slate.com/technology/2013/08/dangers-of-loneliness-social-isolation-is-deadlier-than-obesity.html.

7. Hawkley and Cacioppo, "Loneliness Matters."

8. Olien, "Loneliness Is Deadly."

9. Julianne Holt-Lunstad et al., "Loneliness and Social Isolation as Risk Factors for Mortality: A Meta-Analytic Review," *Perspectives on Psychological Science* 10, no. 2 (2015): 227–237, https://doi.org/10.1177/1745691614568352.

10. "Your Brain Limits You to Just Five BFFs," *MIT Technology Review*, April 29, 2016, https://www.technologyreview.com/s/601369/your-brain-limits-you-to-just-five-bffs/.

11. Dan Buettner, *The Blue Zones*, 2nd ed. (Washington, DC: National Geographic, 2012), 65–120.

12. Cigna Health, *Cigna 2018 U.S. Loneliness Index*, June 4, 2018, https://www.cigna.com/assets/docs/newsroom/loneliness-survey-2018-fact-sheet.pdf.

13. David Ludden, "Does Using Social Media Make You Lonely?" *Psychology Today*, January 24, 2018, https://www.psychologytoday.com/us/blog/talking-apes/201801/does-using-social-media-make-you-lonely.

14. Steve Koppes, "Loneliness Can Make Us More Self-Centered," World Economic Forum, June 21, 2017, https://www.weforum.org/agenda/2017/06/loneliness-can-make-us-make-us-more-self-centred.

15. "Don Lowry and the Lonely Hearts Con Job," KnowledgeNuts, December 6, 2016, https://knowledgenuts.com/2015/12/06/don-lowry-and-the-lonely-hearts-con-job/; Wes Smith, "Knights of Chonda-Za," *Chicago Tribune*, December 19, 1988, https://www.chicagotribune.com/news/ct-xpm-1988-12-19-8802260367-story.html#.

16. Weber, "Psychology's John and Stephanie Cacioppo."

17. Sam Roberts, "John Cacioppo, Who Studied Effects of Loneliness, Is Dead at 66." *New York Times,* March 26, 2018, https://www.nytimes.com/2018/03/26/obituaries/john-cacioppo-who-studied-effects-of-loneliness-is-dead-at-66.html.

18. Roberts, "John Cacioppo."

Creative Freedom

Norman McGuire lives with his wife and four children in a modest home in Apopka, Florida. In the front room of his home, one sees a wall full of exquisite oil paintings and an easel. Norman sits before the easel, palette in his right hand, earbuds filling his mind with inspirational music as he paints. He has been busy; rows of oil paintings lean against the wall several feet deep.

Other than the art studio in the front room, the rest of the household looks typical. Kids fill the den and bedrooms as Norm's wife, Kristin, prepares food. News or sports light up a TV screen, and the dog begs for attention.

From a young age, Norman drew pictures copied from the illustrations in the family's Bible. Art provided a source of comfort for the pain of losing a sister to a tragic accident and the chaos of his father's alcoholism and abuse of his mother. Interestingly, he began to paint around the time his parents divorced.

Being more artist than salesperson, Norman has never turned painting into the booming business it could be. He works as a foreman in a chocolate factory for a paycheck and as a painter for love. It certainly isn't lack of talent that keeps him from worldly success. He paints with a distinct grasp of light and color; some canvases are loaded with details, and others, with one simple scene. He sells only a few paintings, not for lack of buyers but because he wants to keep them together for one yet-future display. You see, each painting illustrates a scene from the life, death, and resurrection of Jesus. Norman is telling Jesus' story on canvas.

I ask Norman a simple question regarding his artwork: What would it do to you to quit creating? He says, "I think about my painting every hour of every day, seven days a week."

His daughter Becky pipes up, "After exhibits, he goes into a mild depression."

Clearly, losing his creative outlet would deflate the man. And so, he paints and paints and paints. And whether he gets paid for it or not, he always will.

I have noticed the same phenomenon in the lives of scores of creative people—musicians, designers, writers, filmmakers, and so on. Some, due to good marketing, good fortune, or both, pull enough money from their crafts to make a living; many don't, potentially dealing a blow to their self-esteem. The moonlighting-as-an-artist life can be extraordinarily difficult to manage in the area of resources. One's energy lags after a day of work, and to summon up new creative ideas, the artist must tap into deep reserves. But to face the routine of life without the artist's craft would deflate him. Yet the individual soldiers on because creativity is as essential to her well-being as the air she breathes.

Creatives

Lest you think one must be an artist or writer to be creative, understand that human creativity is far broader than the arts. In fact, every last one of us is a creative person, whether we realize it or not. The Creator Himself encoded creativity into our DNA when He made us "in His own image" (Genesis 1:27). The Hebrew word for "image" is *tselem,* and it means "representative figure." God created us to represent Him before the cosmos and reveal His character in a way no other creature could. He especially equipped us for that mission by giving us a creative pulse that couldn't be stopped without affecting our life pulse at the same time.

Everyday creativity has been shown to improve well-being: the promotion of "mental health arises by fostering creativity in day to day life."[1] Could it be that the "insane" artist stereotype is wrong? Could creativity enhance mental health rather than harm it? Ruth Richards writes, "Everyday creativity is . . . fundamental to our survival. . . . With our everyday creativity, we adapt flexibly, we improvise, we try different options, whether we are raising a child, counseling a friend, fixing our home, or planning a fundraising event."[2]

It may be that the depression we see in artists and musicians has more to do with being underappreciated and underpaid than the creativity itself.

Everyday creativity traits
1. Openness
2. Flexibility

3. Autonomy
4. Playfulness
5. Humor
6. Willingness to take risks
7. Perseverance[3]

The thought patterns and brain functioning found in mental illness actually counter creativity. In fact, mentally ill creatives probably do their best work when they are asymptomatic. They may create, but research says they probably do so in *spite* of, rather than *because* of, their mental illness.[4] Instead, our imaginativeness fortifies our inner wellness as we fulfill our Creator-given capacity to create—we feel the rush of health as we actualize our true selves. Creativity isn't a sign of illness so much as a sign of health.

Our creative drive is part of the spiritual capacity of human nature. We share many traits with other creatures, such as the ability to bond and play, but only humans have been uniquely equipped with these godlike qualities. Our spiritual capacities are means of self-governance that other creatures who live by instinct don't possess.

In the book *13 Weeks to Peace*, I identified these spiritual capacities as free will, reason, conscience, and faith. I always wondered whether I should have included creativity. This question nagged at me even more because I have been very involved in the arts as a singer, songwriter, and recording artist. The creative impulse that moved so strongly within me begged to be placed somewhere in my own explanation of human nature. What I finally realized—ultimately resolving my dilemma—was that creativity is part of the capacity we call *faith*.

Faith is essentially the ability to believe in and appreciate something we can't discern with our basic senses. We exercise faith toward God and heavenly realities by living in reference to them, even though we can't see, hear, smell, taste, or feel them. This pleases God, because like an earthly father whose children use a graduation-gift smartphone to stay in touch, He sees us using our gifts out of love for Him (Hebrews 11:6). People don't always use their gift of faith to move toward Him, though; many believe a lie (2 Thessalonians 2:11). We may direct our faith as we choose.

God Himself exercises a type of faith in us and our growth process. He "calls into being things that were not" (Romans 4:17, NIV). He molds and fashions us day by day to be more and more attractive, knowing that one day all the rough, ugly edges will be polished away and only beauty will remain. Although that final masterpiece doesn't exist now, God sees it in the future and then mobilizes us to fulfill His dream for us.

In the creative process, we envision a masterpiece that doesn't yet exist, except in our creative imaginations, and then mobilize forces to bring it into existence. This envisioning-into-reality process plays out in every arena of life. We see a potential friendship and visit a neighbor with a loaf of bread. We decide to improve our home, so we budget and plan for beauty and comfort. We organize a family holiday, decorate a kitchen, cook a meal, or choose an outfit. Literally every choice we make can channel God's creative gift into our everyday lives. We constantly call things into existence by envisioning, then working to bring that vision into reality.

The Holy Spirit, who gives life to our spiritual powers, is a divine Person with whom we interact rather than an inanimate power source we co-opt. That Person will lead us to use our spiritual powers in accordance with God's laws, which are the laws of life. It's not that only religious people can be creative; it's that God's Spirit empowers creativity to be used for good and as a blessing. In contrast, creativity used for selfish and destructive purposes represents a misuse of a God-given capacity and won't bring with it the joy and courage that a proper use would. Truly, the enemy of God doesn't really create but only *perverts* God's creations in ways that pass as creativity. "Every good gift and every perfect gift is from above, and comes down from the Father of lights, with whom there is no variation or shadow of turning" (James 1:17).

Life is a canvas

The personality trait that most strongly predicts creativity is *openness to experience*. Openness to experience means curiosity, a love of learning and problem solving, a willingness to ask questions and seek deeper meaning, and engaging emotionally with the world around us. This curiosity factor has more bearing on creative accomplishments than our IQ.

To find out which of the "big five" personality traits you have, see "The 'Big Five' Personality Traits" in the toolbox.

The ability to engage openly with the world involves the neurotransmitter dopamine, which leads a person to seek pleasure and fulfillment. In the brain, dopamine mediates not only pleasure but also the anticipation of pleasure, which can be even more wonderful. God placed this reward-seeking system in our brains to keep us open, curious, and learning throughout life.[5]

Openness to experience

Openness to experience falls into three main categories: intellectual engagement, affective engagement, and aesthetic engagement.

1. *Intellectual engagement* is an interest in "searching for truth, love of problem solving, and drive to engage with ideas."
2. *Affective engagement* is wanting to explore "the full depths of human emotion" and "a preference for using gut feeling, emotions, empathy, and compassion to make decisions."
3. *Aesthetic engagement* is exhibiting "a drive toward exploring fantasy and art" and a tendency to "experience emotional absorption in beauty."

Research has found that intellectual engagement was associated with "creative achievement in the sciences," and "affective and aesthetic engagement were linked with artistic creativity."[6]

For every one of us, life is a canvas. Through the choices we make moment by moment, we sculpt our lives like a work of art. Each one of us is an artist in that sense, and we each will answer for the shape our lives take. Because God has given us free will and, out of that, an infinite number of choices, we bear responsibility for who and what we become.

Many people don't realize this. They feel enslaved to a set of predetermined variables and approach life out of a sense of "I must" rather than "I can." We go forth as if prodded cattle on a slow march toward slaughter. This mind-set makes us less than human, like dumb beasts reacting to our circumstances in thoughtless ways. The resulting suppression of our sense of freedom does violence to our humanity and stifles our potential. The enemy works through various forces to reinforce this sense of enslavement. He builds oppressive human systems, locks people into poverty cycles, leads some into addiction, afflicts many with illness, traumatizes the world through violence and abuse, and generally crushes the human spirit until it is a fraction of itself. Even religion itself stifles freedom when it teaches that God Himself destroys free will by determining all of our choices beforehand.

To be fair, we exercise our God-given freedom in the context of human limitations. The systems, cycles, and events of this world do indeed narrow our options. But while circumstances may confine us in one sense, in another sense, we have a limitless variety of ways we can respond to our circumstances. The enemy attacked Job's family, his fortune, and ultimately, his body, but Job still had the freedom to respond as he so chose. In the same way, the enemy may attack us, but God has put a hedge of protection around the human will, warning the enemy, "Thus far, and no further!"

The human will is sovereign in that we reign over our own volitional center. God has such profound respect for this arrangement that He will not cross the hedge He put in place. Our submission to God is always a chosen submission and never a forced one. As C. S. Lewis wrote, "There are only two kinds of people in the end: those who say to God, 'Thy will be done,' and those to whom God says, in the end, '*Thy* will be done.' "[7] God is so committed to freedom that He will ultimately part with the children He loved unto death rather than force them to live in a heaven they chose to reject.

Amazing brain

The will is housed in the cerebral cortex, the thinking, higher-order part of the brain. Nature protects the brain fiercely; She shields it from harmful chemicals and other invaders through a metabolic and cellular gateway called the blood-brain barrier. She protects it from starvation by allowing energy-filled ketones through that barrier once blood glucose runs out. Because the brain houses our characters, the essence of who we are, God has set many things in place to preserve it. The tragic reality is that we often attack it from the inside. Through developing harmful habits and addictions we compromise brain power and weaken our God-given sovereign wills.

But even then, God has a backup plan. Notice that when Jesus attended a synagogue, a demon-possessed man screeched, "Go away! What do you want with us, Jesus of Nazareth? Have you come to destroy us? I know who you are—the Holy One of God!" (Luke 4:34, NIV). The man had lost his will to the devils that possessed him, and when he opened his mouth to cry out, the devils spoke, but Jesus heard the heart cry of a man who wanted freedom. The poor wretch had lost the ability to cast out his own demons but not the ability to cry out to God for deliverance. Similarly, when we lose power to alcohol, drugs, sex, anger, gossip, fashion, pride, or any other pet sin, the power to cry out to God remains, carefully guarded by the Architect of free will Himself. He puts a fence around our ability to seek Him that nothing can destroy. He says to the enemy, "This far you may come, but no farther" (Job 38:11). We may not be able to fight the enemy, but we can call upon God to fight him for us. This is why the first two steps in the twelve-step recovery process are (1) admitting that we are powerless over our addictions; and (2) believing a power greater than us can restore us to sanity. Alleluia!

An important part of overcoming addiction is reminding ourselves of the power of the will. Our idols deceive us once we pay them obeisance, telling us that we no longer have power. Their lies have such authority because they are partly true: "Don't you know that when you offer yourselves to someone as obedient slaves, you are slaves of the one you obey—whether you are slaves to sin, which leads to death, or to obedience, which leads to righteousness?" (Romans 6:16, NIV). My paraphrase: *When you enslave yourself, you become a slave!* The enemy will do all he can to convince us that we are indeed slaves.

And we are, but that is only part of the story. The rest of the story is that God can restore our ability to choose.

> What you need to understand is the true force of the will. This is the governing power in the nature of man, the power of decision, or of choice. Everything depends on the right action of the will. The power of choice God has given to men; it is theirs to exercise. You cannot change your heart, you cannot of yourself give to God its affections; but you can *choose* to serve Him. You can give Him your will; He will then work in you to will and to do according to His good pleasure. Thus your whole nature will be brought under the control of the Spirit of Christ; your affections will be centered upon Him, your thoughts will be in harmony with Him.[8]

Many things we can't do in our enslaved condition. We can't change our feelings, our temptations, or our desires for our idols. But something remains. We can give God our will. The enemy will steal our will and hold it fast, but the God who created us won't take it without our consent. We must give it to Him. And we can. He preserves that ability, as addicted, habit driven, and helpless as we may be.

Freedom-reminder exercises

Not all bad habits technically qualify as addictions, but the underlying principles of motive and action are the same. We all need a reminder of this wonderful governing power we possess. Sometimes we get lost in the grind of day-to-day life and start to feel as though we are bound by circumstances rather than the masters of them. We do things because we have to, not because we choose to, losing the sense that life is a blank canvas and our own personal creative endeavor. In order to remind ourselves of our innate freedom to choose, we should engage in some pleasant, positive freedom reminders. These can be a very powerful and exhilarating form of self-care.

Think about your daily routine. Now plan a break from it by doing something totally out of the ordinary. Take an evening walk in a different neighborhood. Stop on the way home from work and wade in a splash pool at the park. Purposely choose to buy a different food at the store and prepare it for dinner. Call someone just to say you love him or her. Wear something new, or cut your hair differently.

For more freedom-reminder exercises, see "Freedom-Reminder Exercises" in the toolbox.

Once you realize that you can change your life in small ways, the sense that you have the power to change in big ways will reignite. You can begin to see your life as your canvas. Then you can experience the rekindling of the creative power within you—the agency God has bestowed upon you.

A case study

To grasp how creativity looks in the human experience, let's reflect on the story of a reformed prostitute in the New Testament—Mary of Bethany (commonly identified with Mary Magdalene). She embodies the power of creativity in a way no other disciple did.

Abuse, trauma, unhealthy coping, bad habits, addiction, and finally, demon possession had enslaved this woman in chains of bitterness. In her estrangement from God, she had no more freedom than a beast. Miraculously, through personal interaction with Jesus, through private struggle, and through public failure, she yielded herself fully to Him. God revived her free will and returned it to her to use for His glory and her good.

Mary's gratitude overflowed. She wanted to give her accumulated fortune to the work of the Messiah's teaching and healing, but according to the law, a prostitute's money couldn't be used as an offering (Deuteronomy 23:18). This is where the creative genius of a Spirit-filled believer began to engage.

As Mary considered her options, she recalled that Jesus had foretold His death three times, and the last time He mentioned crucifixion as the means of death (Mark 8:31–33; 9:30–32; 10:33, 34; Matthew 20:17–19). Although Jesus' inner circle of disciples failed to absorb these words, Mary soaked them in like an old towel. She may not have comprehended the breadth of His message, but she thought, *If He is to die, then He must be buried as the King that He is.* A flash of creative genius gave her a unique and wonderful idea. She would use her savings to purchase the most expensive burial ointment possible and would see that Jesus' burial was fit for a king.

Off to the apothecary shop she went, securing an alabaster flask containing spikenard ointment, made from the *Nardostachys jatamansi* flower, harvested from the heights of the Himalayas. The merchants had designed the alabaster flask to open only by breaking, in this way making it an act of extravagant worship for royalty. To make this statement, Mary paid about a year's wages, securing the most expensive gift in town for her Savior.

Mary cherished her flask of ointment, waiting for the right time to anoint her King. Suddenly, she heard He would be crowned after all as a living Monarch over all Judea. Fooled by this wishful thinking, she decided to anoint Him immediately with her precious perfume. He had been invited to Simon the Pharisee's house in honor of Simon's healing from leprosy. Simon was among Mary's abusers, but he was also her uncle. The pain of confronting him notwithstanding, perhaps she would be permitted into the exclusive party as a relative of the host. Hoping her presence would be tolerated, Mary took her ointment to Simon's feast.

She intended to pour it discreetly upon Jesus and leave unnoticed, but she forgot the nearly overpowering spikenard fragrance and the overwhelming joy of her soul delivered from slavery. She wept profusely enough to wash His feet with her tears as the powerful fragrance filled the room with a reminder that this humbly dressed, common-looking Man was the King of all. The disciples noticed and scorned her for her waste. Simon thought evil of her and of Jesus for allowing her near Him. She thought to creep away quietly, but Jesus said, "Leave her alone," then He explained that she had loved Him more than any other (John 12:7; see also Matthew 26:10–13).

Mary's choice brought with it a moment of truth that drew some toward Jesus and pushed others away. Judas left in anger, soon betraying Jesus into the hands of the Sanhedrin. Simon humbled himself and became a steadfast disciple. The spikenard hung in the air of Simon's home and soaked deep into Jesus' skin. The Holy Spirit adorned Mary's creative choice with layers of meaning; her art illustrated the poured-out life of God on the looming cross. Jesus said that wherever the gospel was preached, her story would be told (Matthew 26:13). That has been the case, to be sure.

The following week Jesus rode into Jerusalem on the back of a donkey. Although Jesus looked like a common man, the people worshiped Him. A few days later He hung on the cross, doing what all tortured people do—sweat. Delirious with pain, perhaps Jesus smelled the spikenard fragrance and remembered the woman who loved Him with all of her heart, soul, and creative genius.

Norman McGuire, the artist mentioned in the above story, has a portrait of Mary in the stacks of canvases in his living room. He resonates with her deeply, given their penchants for creating portraits of the cross. And more than this, he understands what it means to pour out everything to tell the story of how Jesus poured out Himself as a creative offering so that we might be "delivered from the bondage of corruption into the glorious liberty of the children of God" (Romans 8:21).

DISCUSSION QUESTIONS

1. Share an example of everyday creativity in your life.

2. Share some examples of everyday creativity in other people's lives.

3. Share the most inspiring work of everyday creativity you have ever encountered.

4. Human beings are made, in the Creator's image, to create. How is creativity linked to faith?

5. How do you remind yourself that your life is a blank canvas?

6. In what sense is the human will sovereign?

7. The enemy can enslave us with addictions and habits, so our freedom is lost. What freedom does God place a hedge around?

8. We need to understand the true force of the will. What can we *not* do with our will? What can we do?

9. How does the story of Mary Magdalene inspire you to take more creative risks?

10. Name three areas in which you can engage in everyday creativity for God's glory.

---

1. Arthur Cropley, "Creativity and Mental Health in Everyday Life," abstract, *Creativity Research Journal* 3, no. 3 (1990), https://doi.org/10.1080/10400419009534351.

2. Ruth Richards, "Everyday Creativity: Our Hidden Potential," in *Everyday Creativity and New Views of Human Nature: Psychological, Social, and Spiritual Perspectives*, ed. Ruth Richards (Washington, DC: American Psychological Association, 2007), 25, 26.

3. Cropley, "Creativity and Mental Health," abstract.

4. Albert Rothenberg, "Creativity and Mental Illness," *Psychology Today*, March 8, 2015, https://www.psychologytoday.com/us/blog/creative-explorations/201503/creativity-and-mental-illness.

5. Scott Barry Kaufman and Carolyn Gregoire, *Wired to Create: Unraveling the Mysteries of the Creative Mind* (New York: TarcherPerigee, 2015), 81–98.

6. Kaufman and Gregoire, *Wired to Create*, 83.

7. C. S. Lewis, *The Great Divorce* (New York: Macmillan, 1946), 69; emphasis in the original.

8. Ellen G. White, *Steps to Christ* (Washington, DC: Review and Herald®, 1956), 47; emphasis in the original.

How May I Help You?

On June 22, 1921, Eva B. Dykes heard her name thunder from the podium at Radcliffe College's commencement ceremony. She walked to center stage as murmurs spread through the hall: Isn't that a black girl? She accepted her diploma and sat down in the spot designated for the seven female doctoral graduates. Eva was the first black American woman to fulfill the requirements for a doctoral degree.

Eva's top-level drive and self-discipline could have launched her into a life of earthly success. It would make sense for her to make a name for herself, breaking the glass ceiling on behalf of other minorities. But Eva had decided long before that she would use all of her gifts to serve the black community. This commitment to service led her down many roads, including giving up her job at the prestigious Howard University in Washington, DC, to teach at Oakwood College in Alabama in 1944. Eva would earn just forty-one dollars a week.[1]

Was she crazy? Why do people pour their talents and riches into the furrow of the world's need? In Eva Dykes's case, deep religious convictions drove her into service. She knew that Jesus left us an example of a poured-out life, dedicating every moment to teaching and healing until He finally made the ultimate sacrifice on the cross. She knew that "the Son of Man did not come to be served, but to serve, and to give His life a ransom for many" (Matthew 20:28). He took "the very nature of a servant" (Philippians 2:7, NIV). She knew that her precious Jesus called her to follow in His footsteps.

Even if we don't have the remarkable energy and talent of Eva Dykes, God calls us to serve one another: "Let each of you look out not only for his own interests, but also for the interests of others" (verse 4). Jesus said, "Whoever desires to become great among you, let him be your servant" (Matthew 20:26). He tells us in Matthew 25:31–46 that in the final reckoning, He will divide the world into unselfish sheep and selfish goats; He will welcome the sheep to eternal bliss and send the goats to eternal condemnation. The difference? The sheep fed, visited, and helped the poor, lonely, and imprisoned, and the goats did not. Great works have flowed from the biblical call to servanthood, giving rise to countless charities, ministries, missions, hospitals, schools, and orphanages. Clearly, God so prioritizes service to others that He makes it a criterion for the final judgment.

Unbelievers get it too

Unbelievers, agnostics, atheists, skeptics, and secular humanists engage in charitable giving and social work too. For example, the biggest online fund-raiser for Doctors Without Borders spontaneously occurred when a group from the atheist community on the website Reddit swarmed Doctors Without Borders's website, bumping the normal four thousand hits per day up to fifty thousand. Donations surged as atheists donated, leaving such comments as "Because god won't," and "Good without god."[2] Foundation Beyond Belief is a humanist community dedicated to advocating "for compassionate action throughout the world." Since launching in 2010, the foundation has formed more than 125 teams that have logged more than one hundred thousand volunteer hours and donated more than two million dollars to other organizations. "There's no supernatural power to make this world a better place. It is up to us," the foundation says.[3] Kiva.org provides microloans to people in seventy-eight nations.[4] In 2011, its most generous contributions came from a team of nonreligious people, and Christian giving trailed behind. Team leader Peter Kroll said, "You either believe the world is in its current state for divine reasons *or* you believe we humans shape the current state of the world. If you believe the latter you're more likely to proactively help to make the world a better place."[5]

In scientific literature, *altruism*—the practice of disinterested and selfless concern for the well-being of others—is heavily correlated with effectiveness and success in the corporate world. A study published years ago in the *Academy of Management Perspectives* states:

The path to profits, it is widely believed, is not paved with caring concern but with Darwinian cleverness. . . .

. . . "Does altruism have a place in our business lives as well as our private lives?

And does it make good economic sense?" The answers may indeed be "yes." For, in reality, parts of the world are proving the opposite of a business paradigm based on self-interest as the pathway to success. For example, the community-based societies of Japan, Taiwan, and Korea are enjoying great economic success. Companies such as the Body Shop donate time and money to environmental welfare projects. Harvard Business School students provide volunteer time to repaint and clean up low-income housing projects. Consumer goods companies change to environment-friendly packaging.[6]

In the end, altruism in corporations fosters prosperity. Companies that practice philanthropy draw better, more conscientious, and more enthusiastic employees and cultivate more customer loyalty. Altruism in leadership predicts employee innovations and teamwork. As children, Torry Holt and his brother Terrence lost their mother to cancer. Torry went on to play football professionally, even being nominated for the Pro Football Hall of Fame. Later, the brothers founded a construction and football company called Holt Brothers, Inc. They also set up a nonprofit corporation to help children who have a parent with cancer. They say, "We don't want our legacy to be only what we accomplished on the football field. Our goal and ambition is to create a competitive, growing company that has the community's best interests at heart."[7]

What motivates service

What motivates believers and unbelievers to serve? While a desire for the applause of others or the approval of God may factor in one's service, the fact is that selfishness isn't all it is cracked up to be. There's a painful vapidity to self-centered living, and a tremendous, deeply felt pleasure involved in a life of service. Behavioral scientists recognize two types of well-being: *hedonic*, which we derive from fun and sensually pleasurable experiences, and *eudemonic*, which comes from a sense of purpose and meaning. Hedonic well-being tends to dissipate quickly, depending upon a constant supply of thrills, whereas eudemonic well-being yields a lasting buzz of deep soul satisfaction. The choice of whether to pursue hedonic or eudemonic pleasure factors into a thousand life choices—whether to enjoy a few nights of sexual freedom or to save oneself for a soulmate or choosing between a big bowl of cholesterol- and sugar-laden ice cream or a healthy bunch of grapes. When someone asked this question on Tumblr, a social networking site, "Anyone know any good substitutes for love and personal fulfillment?" one person replied, "Crunchwrap supreme from taco bell."

That answer may be right but only temporarily. The dopaminergic reward system of the brain sets us up for the pursuit of good feelings. What kind of good feelings we will seek is left to our intelligent-choice-making cerebral cortex.

Serving others produces a natural high. Functional magnetic resonance imaging (fMRI) technology shows how service to others activates the same parts of the brain that are stimulated by food and sex. God wired the capacity for altruism into the brain—and it's immediately pleasurable. But beyond that, it yields a slew of long-term benefits. Let's look at a few:

Better sleep. A study from Northwestern University stumbled upon an unexpected benefit of altruism. Researchers had older participants fill out questionnaires that identified their levels of eudemonic well-being and then compared that with their sleep quality. Those with high levels of meaning and purpose in life were 63 percent less likely to report sleep apnea, 52 percent less likely to have restless leg syndrome, and had moderately better sleep quality overall.[8]

More intelligence. Another study tested memory, executive function, and cognitive function in adults who were thirty-two to eighty-four years old and found that those who possessed an altruistic purpose in life had higher levels of intelligence. This effect applied straight across the board, regardless of age or education level.[9]

Higher self-worth. Researchers studied teens and discovered that eudemonic well-being predicted greater positive self-image, less delinquency, and better transitions into adulthood. This effect was not related to personality type, which means the effect runs deeper than the traits that would normally predict those things. In science, this is a very strong effect![10]

Longevity. In a large-scale, global study, eudemonic well-being correlated with longevity, meaning that, in general, the more altruistic purpose people had, the longer they lived.[11] Another study specified that at least two hours per week of volunteering, stretched out over many years, reduces one's mortality rate by nearly 40 percent.[12]

Happier children. Did you know that children are actually happier giving than receiving? A group from the University of British Columbia nailed that down. When children associate unselfish giving with the "warm glow" feeling that accompanies it, they learn to love it. Amazingly, they enjoy "costly giving"—giving that requires personal sacrifice—even more than giving that doesn't.[13] (I seem to recall Jesus saying something about learning from children.)

More resilience. Researchers assessed college students who took immersion trips to serve in poor and marginalized communities at home and overseas. The researchers checked the students' levels of desirable traits, such as resilience and compassion. These students had more of these positive traits and managed stress better over time than the control group who hadn't taken such a trip.[14]

Stress management. Entering into the plight of other people and helping them pulls our focus away from our worries. Just taking the trip from self to others can open a way of escape from the hamster-wheel cycles of personal pressure. In the words of Alice Walton, serving others "takes the focus off ourselves, which seems to be health-giving in more ways than one. Much of our mental anguish, stress and depression is linked to rumination and worry-based, self-referential thoughts."[15]

Here's a powerful description of the psychological impact of service to others:

> Many are in obscurity. They have lost their bearings. They know not what course to pursue. Let the perplexed ones search out others who are in perplexity and speak to them words of hope and encouragement. When they begin to do this work, the light of heaven will reveal to them the path that they should follow. By their words of consolation to the afflicted they themselves will be consoled. By helping others, they themselves will be helped out of their difficulties. Joy takes the place of sadness and gloom. The heart, filled with the Spirit of God, glows with warmth toward every fellow being. Every such a one is no longer in darkness; for his "darkness" is "as the noon day."[16]

Joy is a matter of stewardship

Speaking now as a person who reads these types of studies often—this list could go on and on! The number of benefits of service is off the charts. For health's sake, for life's sake, we need to get busy and help other people.

> Doing good is a work that benefits both giver and receiver. If you forget self in your interest for others, you gain a victory over your infirmities. . . .

The pleasure of doing good animates the mind and vibrates through the whole body.[17]

Do you feel bad? Help someone else, and you will feel better.

Some may think that seeking good feelings at all is selfish and the idea of living a life of service for happiness's sake sounds like being unselfish for selfish reasons. I propose we see it as a matter of stewardship. God has given us our lives to manage and govern. Choosing a life course that will encourage a positive psychological state is just good, responsible supervision of God's gift of life. Because long-term negative emotions have negative health consequences, encouraging positive emotions is not different in principle from eating a high-fiber diet. It's selfish to idolize happiness but not selfish to seek it with the motive of caring for ourselves as part of God's creation.

It's selfish to put our temporary happiness before the needs of other people but not selfish to prioritize our long-term happiness at a high level for the sake of being able to serve others better.

Giving without expecting anything in return is a beautiful thing. A life that spills over for the good of all portrays the heart of God. But let's face it, none of us starts there. In our self-interest, we seek better health, stumbling upon eternal principles of right living. Once we adopt this better way of life, we develop a taste for it. We may begin serving others because it gives us good feelings and good health, but God can take us from there into the deeper, more internalized motives of serving sacrificially. Once we see the very real impact we can make upon the lives of others and the connected nature of the human brotherhood, service becomes reflexive.

Would you like to revise your life purpose to include more service to others? Look for "My Personal Mission Statement" in the toolbox. Would you like to become more effective at setting and achieving goals? "Goal Setting" in the toolbox may help. Would you like to improve your overall health through better habits? "Twelve Good Habits" and "Good Habit Inventory" in the toolbox may help.

How to get started

In Matthew 25:14–30, Jesus told a parable about a wealthy investor who gave various amounts of money to his traders, hoping for a good return on his investment. To one, he gave the equivalent of $1.5 million; to a second trader, he gave $600,000; and to a third,

$300,000.[18] The investor left on an extended vacation. When he returned, the first and second traders had doubled his assets, but the third had buried them in the ground, afraid of financial loss and the disapproval of the investor. Enraged, the investor called the trader "wicked and lazy," took his money away, gave it to the others, and commanded that the "unprofitable servant" be cast "into the outer darkness" where "there will be weeping and gnashing of teeth" (verses 26, 30).

Through this rather startling parable, Jesus meant to communicate something very helpful to those who have little: You are not off the hook! A nicer way of saying this is don't underestimate the power of small offerings. The widow gave her mites, and the world stopped to notice. The lowly volunteer may be doing more than the philanthropist donating millions.

The reason the sacrifices of the poor matter more than the donations of the rich is that God partners with us in the giving, working on the principle of multiplication. We give 5, and He multiplies it by 5, making 25. We give that 25 back, and He multiplies it by that, making it 625. We give back that 625, and He multiplies it by 625, making it 390,625. See how fast multiplication grows things? That's how investing works in the heavenly market. But God multiplies *sacrificial* offerings. "Do not forget to do good and to share, for with such sacrifices God is well pleased" (Hebrews 13:16). In this verse, "sacrifices" refers to the sacrificial lamb of the sanctuary, which was a symbol of the sacrifice Jesus would make in pouring out His life on the cross. Jesus offered Himself through the eternal Spirit (Hebrews 9:14). The same Spirit works with our infinitely lesser sacrifices today.

Sacrificing quietly

The Live Aid concerts in 1985—with famous performances by Queen, Bob Dylan, David Bowie, and scores of other rock superstars—raised $127 million for famine relief in Ethiopia. We would like to think that such large sums would turn around the fortunes of a devastated nation. Some argue that Live Aid and the many similar enterprises that followed really helped. But other people, even within the music industry, point out that corrupt government systems that rob their own citizens will also steal and misuse money donated to help them. Without boots-on-the-ground effort to change the way people and societies function, money can actually do more harm than good.[19] Do the celebrities involved in such enterprises sacrifice? Maybe, but not to the point of putting a dent in their fortunes, which are well into the hundreds of millions. This isn't to fault them for doing *something* to help the less fortunate. It's to point out that the most effective servants have always been the droves of simple, average people who sacrifice quietly in order to make a difference. Given that the majority of those reading this book are just such people, I am trying to help us recognize our significance.

Film director Tom Shadyac became wealthy through his work with such movies as *Ace Ventura: Pet Detective*, *The Nutty Professor*, and *Liar, Liar*, only to sell off most of his possessions, including a seventeen-thousand-square-foot mansion in Los Angeles and devote his life to humanitarianism. He dedicated the funds to charity, and in 2010, he released the documentary *I Am*, which explores human connectedness, happiness, and the world's addiction to materialism.

It turns out that true success is loving, being loved, and serving others.

DISCUSSION QUESTIONS

1. What do you think motivates unbelievers to engage in service to others?

2. At what moment in your life did you feel the greatest eudemonic well-being?

3. What about altruism helps corporations that encourage it to flourish?

4. Is it selfish to try to feel good? Why, or why not?

5. Although we may begin serving others out of a desire to be healthy and feel good, what will God do from there?

6. Can we develop a habit of serving others? If so, how?

7. What is the difference between giving and sacrificial giving?

8. What is Jesus' message to those with very little of this world's goods?

9. What kept the "unprofitable servant" from investing his employer's money? How does that relate to us today?

10. What is your definition of true success? What would it look in your life?

---

1. For more about Eva B. Dykes, see DeWitt S. Williams, "Eva Beatrice Dykes: First African American Woman to Complete PhD Requirements," *Spectrum*, December 10, 2018, https://spectrummagazine.org/news/2018/eva-beatrice-dykes-first-african-american-woman-complete-phd-requirements.

2. Tom Miles, "Irreverent Atheists Crowdsource Charitable Giving," Reuters, December 12, 2011, https://www.reuters.com/article/us-atheists-donations/irreverent-atheists-crowdsource-charitable-giving-idUSTRE7B81SU20111212.

3. "Mission and Accomplishments," Foundation Beyond Belief, accessed June 17, 2019, https://foundationbeyondbelief.org/inside-fbb/about/mission/.

4. "About," Kiva, accessed June 17, 2019, https://www.kiva.org/about.

5. Peter Kroll, quoted in Hank Pellissier, "Atheists Are the Most Generous—Even Without Heavenly Reward," Institute for Ethics and Emerging Technologies, November 25, 2011, https://ieet.org/index.php/IEET2/more/pellissier20111125.

6. Rabindra N. Kanungo and Jay A. Conger, "Promoting Altruism as a Corporate Goal," abstract, *Academy of Management Perspectives* 7, no. 3 (1993), https://doi.org/10.5465/ame.1993.9411302345.

7. "Home," Holt Brothers, accessed June 17, 2019, http://holtbrothersinc.com.

8. Arlener D. Turner, Christine E. Smith, and Jason C. Ong, "Is Purpose in Life Associated With Less Sleep Disturbance in Older Adults?" *Sleep Science and Practice* 1, no. 14 (2017), https://doi.org/10.1186/s41606-017-0015-6.

9. Nathan A. Lewis et al., "Purpose in Life and Cognitive Functioning in Adulthood," *Aging, Neuropsychology, and Cognition* 24, no. 6 (2017): 662–671, https://doi.org/10.1080/13825585.2016.1251549.

10. Patrick L. Hill et al., "Purpose in Life in Emerging Adulthood: Development and Validation of a New Brief Measure," abstract, *Journal of Positive Psychology* 11, no. 3 (2016), https://doi.org/10.1080/17439760.2015.1048817.

11. Andrew Steptoe, Angus Deaton, and Arthur A. Stone, "Subjective Wellbeing, Health, and Ageing," *Lancet* 385, no. 9968 (2015): 640–648, https://doi.org/10.1016/S0140-6736(13)61489-0.

12. Alex H. S. Harris and Carl E. Thoresen, "Volunteering Is Associated With Delayed Mortality in Older People: Analysis of the Longitudinal Study of Aging," *Journal of Health Psychology* 10, no. 6 (2005): 739–752, https://doi.org/10.1177/1359105305057310.

13. Lara B. Aknin, J. Kiley Hamlin, and Elizabeth W. Dunn, "Giving Leads to Happiness in Young Children," *PLoS ONE* 7, no. 6 (2012), https://doi.org/10.1371/journal.pone.0039211.

14. Thomas G. Plante, Katy Lackey, and Jeong Yeon Hwang, "The Impact of Immersion Trips on Development of Compassion Among College Students," *Journal of Experiential Education* 32, no. 1 (2009): 29–43, https://doi.org/10.1177/105382590903200104.

15. Alice G. Walton, "The Science of Giving Back: How Having a Purpose Is Good for Body and Brain," *Forbes*, July 10, 2017, https://www.forbes.com/sites/alicegwalton/2017/07/10/the-science-of-giving-back-how-having-a-purpose-is-good-for-body-and-brain/.

16. Ellen G. White, *Mind, Character, and Personality*, vol. 2 (Nashville: Southern Pub. Assn., 1977), 431, 432.

17. Ellen G. White, *Messages to Young People* (Nashville: Southern Pub. Assn., 1930), 209.

18. There are a number of different opinions about the equivalents of a talent in today's currency. Arland Hultgren writes that a talent is about six thousand denarii, with a denarius being a day's wages for a working man. If a working man makes (a very conservative) fifty dollars a day, six thousand denarii would be three hundred thousand dollars. Arland Hultgren, *The Parables of Jesus: A Commentary* (Grand Rapids, MI: Eerdmans, 2000), 23.

19. Robert Keating, "Live Aid: The Terrible Truth," *Spin*, July 1986, repr. July 13, 2015, https://www.spin.com/featured/live-aid-the-terrible-truth-ethiopia-bob-geldof-feature/.

Thank God for Gratitude

Sweet, gentle Esther had come to the United States from Barbados to study nursing. She had finished her studies and found herself a decent job. Unfortunately, it was at an intensive care unit where they had a 50 percent death rate. When the lack of sunlight in the unit, death all around, loneliness in a new country, and many traumas and disappointments of her life compounded into depression, she reached out to me.

When I realize someone is headed down the depression spiral, I can become quite direct. I urged Esther to try a series of measures to improve her mood in hopes she would bounce out of it: "Try a hot and cold shower every day. They use hot and cold in Germany to treat depression," I said, "and get a happy light to increase your brain serotonin. You need to get regular exercise—walking is fine—but get it regularly and make sure you sweat a little, if possible." Then, almost as an afterthought, I said: "Oh, and each day write down three things you are grateful for, and share each one with at least one other person."

It was months before I talked to Esther again, but when I did, she reported with tears of joy that her life had turned around. She was socializing freely, taking care of her health, being honest and vulnerable with people, having devotions in the morning, and just generally enjoying life. Then she dropped the bomb: "Between the ages of seventeen and twenty-five, I prayed *every day* to die. I didn't want to kill myself because I was Catholic, and believed I would burn in hell forever if I did. But I wanted out. Life was just too hard. This weekend I turned thirty. And I realized that I was *grateful* I made it to thirty years old. I spent almost ten years wishing I could die; now I am grateful to be alive. I never thought I would get here."

Esther thanked me again and again for assigning the gratitude exercise. It had made all the difference for her. I silently kicked myself for almost forgetting it, for not assigning it more often, and for not practicing it myself as much as I should.

The many benefits of gratitude

Joel Wong and Joshua Brown from Indiana University wanted to find some biggest-bang-for-the-buck homework for counseling clients, so they ran an experiment on just under three hundred students who were seeking help for serious anxiety and depression from a university counseling clinic. These weren't high-functioning, healthy, "together" people finding ways to feel even better but seriously depressed and anxious students needing a lifeline—or else.

Wong and Brown split the students into three groups. The first (control) group simply received counseling. In addition to counseling, the second group wrote out their deepest thoughts and feelings about negative experiences, and the third group wrote one letter of gratitude to another person each week for three weeks.

All three groups received counseling, but only one group expressed gratitude. The researchers checked after four weeks and again at twelve weeks, and both times the gratitude group reported "significantly better mental health" than the other two groups.[1] This may seem like a small thing, but in science, *significantly* is a very weighty word. For the third group to have improvement even months after merely writing three letters of gratitude is mind-blowing. To so radically impact a person's mental health with an intervention that costs no money and little time is the stuff of legend.

It's not just mental health that gratitude impacts. Grateful people are *physically* healthier. "Nothing tends to promote health of body and of soul than does a spirit of gratitude and praise."[2] One study showed that not only does gratitude itself yield health benefits, but grateful people tend to care for their bodies more faithfully.[3]

Another study showed that grateful people are more relationally healthy. Something as simple as thanking a new acquaintance for being helpful incentivizes that person to seek a future relationship. "Saying thank you provides a valuable signal that you are someone with whom a high-quality relationship could be formed."[4]

Grateful people even sleep better. Several studies have shown this, including one involving more than four hundred adult participants who completed questionnaires about gratitude, sleep, and presleep thoughts. Researchers found that the more grateful people were at bedtime, the faster they dozed off and the longer they slept.[5]

Once grateful people get up to face the world, they feel better about themselves. Grateful athletes have been shown to have higher self-esteem, which is important to good athletic performance, when they also have trusting relationships with their coaches. How about bouncing back from trauma? Grateful Vietnam War veterans "experienced lower levels of post-traumatic stress disorder." One study showed that "gratitude was a major contributor to resilience following the terrorist attacks on September 11."[6]

There's more. Wong and Brown also learned about the *how* of the gratitude effect. The *displacement effect*, which shifts

For a series of gratitude exercises, see "Gratitude 101" in the toolbox. For a meditation technique that incorporates gratitude, see "Gratitude Meditation" in the toolbox.

one's thinking away from negative thoughts, appears to be part of gratitude's potency because the people who saw the greatest effect used the fewest negative words in their writing. Gratitude also blooms slowly, increasing in effect rather than diminishing as many therapy exercises tend to do.[7]

A now-famous study by Robert Emmons and Michael McCullough showed similar results. In their study, "one group wrote about things they were grateful for," a second group "wrote about daily irritations," and a "third wrote about events that had affected them," negative or positive. The researchers found that the gratitude group not only raised their optimism levels but also exercised more! Gratitude opens the heart's motivational springs and self-care impulses. Martin Seligman similarly tested a group, asking participants to complete writing assignments. For those asked to write a letter of gratitude to someone who'd never been properly thanked, happiness scores soared, the impact outstripping any other intervention and lasting a full month.[8]

Gratitude has been identified in social-science studies as helping people to feel better, but recent research by C. Nathan DeWall and his coauthors shows that gratitude helps people to *be* better. Their study reports that "gratitude motivates people to express sensitivity and concern for others and stimulates prosocial behavior. Aggression . . . runs counter to the motivation to increase others' welfare and should be reduced among grateful people." Gratitude cultivates what DeWall calls a "nonviolent heart" in people.[9] Gratitude infuses us with empathy, which counteracts our aggressive, selfish impulses. We can't evangelize and antagonize at the same time. We can't be curious and angry at the same time. We can't empathize and aggress at the same time. Gratitude introduces dynamics and emotions that snuff out our baser instincts, making room for goodwill to flourish.

This may be why God so often tells us to praise Him and give thanks. More than 250 times, He commands us to praise Him, and the Bible mentions thanksgiving more than fifty times. Although God didn't mention praise and thanksgiving explicitly in the Ten Commandments, could it be that obeying the commands to praise and thank Him will help fuel our obedience to the written-in-stone Ten? Could it be that a lifestyle of grateful praise turns our sinful nature out of its course, creating space for the Spirit of God to energize and transform us?

Lest we relegate the benefits of gratitude to naturally grateful people, DeWall shoots holes in that myth, showing how even an occasional habit of counting one's blessings or writing a gratitude letter can shape the character toward these virtues. There is a place for anger, even aggression. We can't be angels all the time. But even the grumpiest of us can benefit from some gratitude practices. Gratitude isn't only for the sweet little old ladies and exuberant children among us. It's for the pressured CEO, the wizened old curmudgeon, and the street-smart tough guy. Just a little bit of gratitude here and there will soften even the hardest cases.

How do we miss something so powerful yet so simple? Gratitude is like the brain-recharging fresh air that would pour in and revitalize us if we would only open the window; it's the simple, inexpensive food that would nourish our bodies if we would only eat it. It's always there, always available, free of charge, and often forgotten.

So consider this chapter a reminder.

Summary of the benefits of gratitude
1. It helps us to make friends.
2. It makes us healthier.
3. It helps us to sleep.
4. It makes us nicer.
5. It helps our self-worth.
6. It helps us to recover from trauma.

Giving credit

So how can we make the shift to a life of gratitude? Being mindful of good things comes as a result of a choice on our part. Paul tells us that "whatever is true, whatever is noble, whatever is right, whatever is pure, whatever is lovely, whatever is admirable—if anything is excellent or praiseworthy—think about such things" (Philippians 4:8, NIV). *Logizomai*, the word for "think about such things," means to give credit for something. The Bible uses this word or its Hebrew equivalent close to one hundred times! Apparently, we have to be reminded to give credit to God and others who deserve acknowledgment because we take them for granted. When we eliminate the positive from our thoughts, speech, and prayers, in a sense, we fail to make good on a debt for all that has gone well. So our lifestyle change from negativity to gratitude involves intentionality—a focused, purposeful effort to cultivate the habit of dwelling on the true, noble, just, pure, and lovely.

We shouldn't be discouraged if we have to make this effort again and again. We may have to revisit our gratitude commitment from time to time, getting back on the praise wagon, so to speak. But the good news is that habits revisited over and over will eventually stick. "That which at first seems difficult, by constant repetition grows easy, until right thoughts and actions become habitual."[10] We human beings will often start a new practice, lose momentum after a while, and backslide. This is actually typical human behavior, not something only hopeless cases do. There's no need to conclude, "Well, I tried that, and I just couldn't stick to it." Start over!

> Watch your thoughts; they become words;
> watch your words; they become actions;
> watch your actions; they become habits;
> watch your habits; they become character;
> watch your character; for it becomes your destiny.[11]

Perceived value syndrome

Dating and marriage experts have noticed that a failure to find a suitable life partner can sometimes be based on what basically is inverted covetousness. They have named this pattern *perceived value syndrome* because it leads a person to strive for self-enrichment but in a dysfunctional, unproductive way. Desire in and of itself can be from God, ultimately leading us to Him, the Desire of Ages. But in perceived value syndrome, desire takes a sharp turn toward selfishness. It looks something like this: Julie loves Mack until Mack loves Julie, and then Julie stops loving Mack until Mack walks off in a huff and starts talking to other girls, at which point Julie loves Mack again. Mack remains charming, good looking, and desirable throughout; the only changing variable is his availability. When available, his perceived value to Julie descends; when not, it rises. And on and on and on. Perceived value syndrome is a self-defeating aversion to what is available simply because it's available.

Pop psychology says, "Well, Julie needs self-esteem work. She thinks that any man who loves her must not be a valuable man, so she rejects him." But I wonder. If her self-esteem is so low, why does she want a valuable man at all? I'm not denying that low self-esteem leads some Julies of the world to choose low-life guys; I'm simply questioning whether low self-esteem is behind perceived value syndrome. After all, Julie is trying to acquire something of value; this doesn't look like low self-esteem at all.

Actually, perceived value syndrome flows out of our naturally high self-esteem, or at least, our desire to have high self-esteem. Perceived value syndrome, at its core, is covetousness. We traditionally understand covetousness as wanting other people's stuff. But the flip side of it is just as dark—it's not wanting our stuff.

The commandment says, "You shall not covet your neighbor's house; you shall not covet your neighbor's wife, nor his male servant, nor his female servant, nor his ox, nor his donkey, nor anything that is your neighbor's" (Exodus 20:17). The longing for what God hasn't given reduces one's gratitude for what God has given. The moment a man starts coveting the wife, marriage, family, income, ministry, house, garden, and/or dog of his neighbor, he fails to cherish his own wife, marriage, family, income, ministry, house, garden, and/or dog. Covetousness and ingratitude sustain a symbiotic relationship with one another, keeping each other fed and happy like an Egyptian plover bird picking leeches off the gums of a Nile crocodile.

We may try to stop coveting cold turkey, but we must find a replacement behavior or be doomed to relapse. Behavioral scientists point out that negative reinforcement temporarily stops a behavior, but positive reinforcement must be given in order to sustain a change long-term. God always gives us something better to wean us off the bad. In the case of covetousness, the replacement behavior is gratitude. To quote the songwriter Sheryl Crow: "It's not having what you want, it's wanting what you've got."[12] Wanting what we have is the antidote to our endless greed for more. Perhaps the reason God commands us over and over to thank Him is that it weans us off our poverty mind-set, our desperate grasping for self-enrichment, to a place of contentment.

The covetous core

The apostle Paul intimated that the prohibition on covetousness was the commandment he struggled the most to keep. This makes sense given that Paul had grown up under strict Jewish training and possessed a powerful, disciplined will that made behavioral compliance easy to him. All the commandments involve the observation of external behaviors with the exception of the tenth—covetousness—and the obedience to this commandment can't be manufactured, forced, or faked. This commandment demands a change of heart. This unsettled Paul, who cried, "I would not have known covetousness unless the law had said, 'You shall not covet.' But sin, taking opportunity by the commandment, produced in me all manner of evil desire. For apart from the law sin was dead. I was alive once without the law, but when the commandment came, sin revived and I died. And the commandment, which was to bring life, I found to bring death. For sin, taking occasion by the commandment, deceived me, and by it killed me" (Romans 7:7–11). Notice the language: "I died," "it killed me." This man is struggling for his sanity. And the core issue? Covetousness, or wanting what others had.

Author Ellen White expands this idea: "Paul says that 'as touching the law,'—as far as outward acts were concerned,—he was 'blameless,' but when the spiritual character of the law was discerned, when he looked into the holy mirror, he saw himself a sinner. Judged by a human standard, he had abstained from sin, but when he looked into the depths of God's law, and saw himself as God saw him, he bowed in humiliation, and confessed his guilt."[13]

Let's think about this for a moment. What's the difference between wanting what one doesn't have and not wanting what one does have? Nothing, substantially; one is the flip side of the other. These are two tributaries in a never-ending feedback loop where one dysfunction leads to the next, which refuels the former, which feeds the latter—and on and on and on. Each unhealthy dynamic flows into and recharges the next.

Sin began when an honored angel, inexplicably and irrationally, began to covet. Lucifer, wise and beautiful, covered with jewels and privilege, wanted the one thing he didn't have—God's status. "Your heart was lifted up because of your beauty; you corrupted your wisdom for the sake of your splendor" (Ezekiel 28:17).

"For you have said in your heart:
'I will ascend into heaven,
I will exalt my throne above the stars of God;
I will also sit on the mount of the congregation
On the farthest sides of the north;
I will ascend above the heights of the clouds,
I will be like the Most High' " (Isaiah 14:13, 14).

"Though all his glory was from God, this mighty angel came to regard it as pertaining to himself. Not content with his position, though honored above the heavenly host, he ventured to covet homage due alone to the Creator. Instead of seeking to make God supreme in the affections and allegiance of all created beings, it was his endeavor to secure their service and loyalty to himself. And coveting the glory with which the infinite Father had invested His Son, this prince of angels aspired to power that was the prerogative of Christ alone."[14]

Forgetting his status as a created being, Lucifer became inflated in his self-assessment. The fact that he lacked the status of the Creator rendered his pride a withering blow. In a compensatory effort, he redirected the affections and worship of the angels to himself, becoming a self-appointed deity on a mission to rob God of the honor due Him. He murdered God's reputation, committed spiritual adultery, stole the honor due to God, and lied to himself and others. Every broken commandment is traceable back to the slippery, intangible, but high-impact twist of the mind we call covetousness.

Lucifer has threaded human history with covetousness: nation rising up against nation, ambition colliding with ambition, and the annals of time literally throbbing with inordinate longing. According to prophecy, the last days of the earth's history will bring forth a religious-political institution bearing, as no earthly power has before, a most malevolent form of covetousness. This "man of sin," as he is called, "opposes and exalts himself above all that is called God or that is worshiped, so that he sits as God in the temple of God, showing himself that he is God" (2 Thessalonians 2:3, 4). That same megalomaniacal greed that would tear God off His throne will come oozing forth, prideful, arrogant, entitled, and covetous to the core to demand that the world follow in its ungrateful steps.

We can move in precisely the opposite direction by falling at the feet of Jesus in gratitude. Lucifer, a created being, grasped for the privileges, power, and prerogatives of God. God the Creator surrendered His privileges, power, and prerogatives to the Cross. Ultimately, we will follow the example of one or the other. While discipline and techniques, such as some of the ones mentioned here, may help in our journey from natural covetousness to gratitude, the power behind that choice is in beholding the love of God. Jesus "made Himself of no reputation, taking the form of a bondservant, and coming in the likeness of men. And being found in appearance as a man, He humbled Himself and became obedient to the point of death, even the death of the cross" (Philippians 2:7, 8). Instead of grasping for more, He let go of all. Of course, He remained God throughout the death experience, but in terms of what He felt and experienced in those harrowing hours, He lost everything, including His bond with the Father. If not for this sacrifice, He couldn't have given us the riches of eternity. "Though He was rich, yet for your sakes He became poor, that you through His poverty might become rich" (2 Corinthians 8:9). The sheer generosity of the gift inspires His followers to sing, "Worthy is the Lamb who was slain to receive power and riches and wisdom, and strength and honor and glory and blessing!" (Revelation 5:12).

DISCUSSION QUESTIONS

1. Some of the positive effects of gratitude come from the fact that it displaces negativity. What percentage of your thought life would you estimate is negative?

2. Gratitude not only makes us feel better but also makes us better people, infusing us with empathy. Have you experienced the character-softening effects of gratitude? If so, how?

3. Why do you think God asks us to praise Him, effectively giving Him credit for His works?

4. What if we start living more grateful lives and fall off the wagon? Then what?

5. Do you relate to perceived value syndrome? Have you struggled with wanting what you don't have and not wanting what you do have?

6. Longing for what God hasn't given reduces the gratitude for what God has given. How have you experienced this?

7. Covetousness began when Lucifer did what?

8. In what area of your life do you struggle the most with covetousness?

9. How does it affect you to know that while Lucifer grasped for the privileges, power, and prerogatives of God, God in Christ surrendered His privileges, power, and prerogatives to the Cross?

10. What about God's character provokes the most gratitude in your heart?

1. Joel Wong and Joshua Brown, "How Gratitude Changes You and Your Brain," *Greater Good Magazine,* June 6, 2017, https://greatergood.berkeley.edu/article/item/how_gratitude_changes_you_and_your_brain.

2. Ellen G. White, *The Ministry of Healing* (Mountain View, CA: Pacific Press®, 1952), 251.

3. Patrick Hill, Mathias Allemand, and Brent Roberts, "Examining the Pathways Between Gratitude and Self-Rated Physical Health Across Adulthood," *Personality and Individual Differences* 54, no. 1 (January 2013): 92–96, https://doi.org/10.1016/j.paid.2012.08.011.

4. Lisa A. Williams and Monica Y. Bartlett, "Warm Thanks: Gratitude Expression Facilitates Social Affiliation in New Relationships via Perceived Warmth," *Emotion* 15, no. 1 (2015): 1–5, https://doi.org/10.1037/emo0000017.

5. Alex M. Wood et al., "Gratitude Influences Sleep Through the Mechanism of Pre-sleep Cognitions," *Journal of Psychosomatic Research* 66, no. 1 (January 2009): 43–48, https://doi.org/10.1016/j.jpsychores.2008.09.002.

6. Amy Morin, "7 Scientifically Proven Benefits of Gratitude," *Psychology Today*, April 3, 2015, https://www.psychologytoday.com/us/blog/what-mentally-strong-people-dont-do/201504/7-scientifically-proven-benefits-gratitude.

7. Wong and Brown, "How Gratitude Changes You."

8. Harvard Health Publishing staff, "In Praise of Gratitude," *Harvard Mental Health Letter*, last updated June 5, 2019, https://www.health.harvard.edu/mind-and-mood/in-praise-of-gratitude.

9. C. Nathan DeWall et al., "A Grateful Heart Is a Nonviolent Heart: Cross-Sectional, Experience Sampling, Longitudinal, and Experimental Evidence," *Social Psychological and Personality Science* 3, no. 2 (2012): 323–240, https://doi.org/10.1177/1948550611416675.

10. White, *The Ministry of Healing*, 491.

11. Frank Outlaw, untitled poem, What They're Saying, *San Antonio Light*, May 18, 1977, 7B.

12. Sheryl Crow, "Soak Up the Sun," track 2 on *C'mon, C'mon*, A&M Records, 2001–2002.

13. Ellen G. White, " 'Go and Tell Him His Fault Between Thee and Him Alone,' " *Advent Review and Sabbath Herald*, July 22, 1890, 450.

14. Ellen G. White, *Patriarchs and Prophets* (Oakland, CA: Pacific Press®, 1890), 35.

The Mighty Power of Awed

In her book *Confessions of a Christian Wife*, Heather Thompson Day recalls a moment of God-inspired awe that changed the course of her life. Although her wedding was two months away, with the invitations and dress already purchased, Heather wrestled with doubts. So did her parents. One evening she prayed, "Lord, this is the person that I have chosen; but if he isn't the person that You have chosen for me, please end it."

Two minutes later, the phone rang, and her fiancé broke up with her.

"I laid lifeless in my bed that evening. . . . I could swear that that wedding dress hanging in my closet kept poking its head out and laughing at me," she writes. Later that same night, a miserable Heather prayed again—this time begging for mercy. Her phone rang again. It was Seth Day.

Seth Day, her sixth-grade crush. Seth Day, the tan boy with blue eyes who had passed her notes in class. Seth Day, whose family moved away after the seventh grade but who reemerged at her college as an adult. She had written her number on a scrap of paper and slipped it to him but later realized he had a "pretty, little blond girlfriend." Soon Heather started dating the man who would become her fiancé, and her dreams of Seth faded away into the drama of that relationship.

Seth had saved the number she gave him—he had "folded it and tucked it into his backpack." It sat there for two years, through the breakup of his relationship with the pretty blond girl, and after that, he would take out the paper, unfold it, start to dial the number, then remember that Heather had someone, and hang up. However, the night her engagement ended, as she cried out for mercy on her bed, Seth suddenly, inexplicably, decided to call. He said, "Heather . . . Hey, I'm not really sure why I am calling. I just felt like I should."

It was a moment of pure, unalloyed, divine-interposition-fueled awe. Like a supernatural symphony, God's perfectly timed intervention fell right on the beat. Heather ended up marrying the blue-eyed boy from her sixth-grade class. She says that sometimes fairy tales come "wrapped in closed doors, fake smiles, and sleepless nights."[1]

Most of us don't have stories as miraculous as Heather's, but we have moments of awe—moments when the divine touches our humanity in such a stark way that we stop breathing for a moment. Webster's dictionary defines *awe* as "fear mixed with dread, veneration, reverence, or wonder" that is "inspired by something sacred, mysterious, or morally impressive."[2] All of us have encountered the sacred or sublime—a magnificent waterfall, a moment of comfort in sadness, or the birth of a child. God regularly makes house calls to us human beings if we will but answer the door.

In awe of awe

Awe: Sigmund Freud called it "oceanic feelings"; Abraham Maslow identified it as "peak experiences."[3] Albert Einstein said, "The most beautiful thing we can experience is the mysterious. It is the source of all true art and science. He to whom this emotion is a stranger, who can no longer pause to wonder and stand rapt in awe, is as good as dead: his eyes are closed."[4]

Dacher Keltner, the director of the Berkeley Social Interaction Laboratory at the University of California, Berkeley, says, "Awe is the feeling of being in the presence of something vast that transcends your understanding of the world."[5]

Dr. Keltner is convinced that regular experiences of awe improve us morally. In one experiment he and a colleague conducted, "participants first either looked up into the tall trees for one minute—long enough for them to report being filled with awe"—or looked "at the facade of a large science building." They then watched a staged person stumble, "dropping a handful of pens into the dirt." Keltner wanted to see if the awe-filled participants would be kinder. They were. The participants who had been gazing up at the awe-inspiring trees picked up more pens. Awe seemed to increase the participants' inclination "to help someone in need. They also reported feeling less entitled and self-important than the other study participants did." Awe humbled them and made them better people.[6]

Keltner and his team once gave fifteen hundred people a questionnaire on awe. Next, they gave each participant ten lottery tickets that could be entered for a cash prize and then invited them to share the tickets with other people who had not received any tickets. The participants who had more wonder and appreciation of beauty in their daily experience gave away more tickets.[7]

In another study, Dr. Keltner's colleague Michelle Shiota had participants stand before either an awe-inspiring replica of a *T. rex* in UC Berkeley's Museum of Paleontology or turn around and look down a hallway.[8] Then they filled in the blank in the statement "I am ____." When the participants looked at the awe-inspiring creature, they more often defined themselves "in collectivist terms—as a member of a culture, a species, a university, or a moral cause. Awe embeds the individual self in a social identity."[9]

Awe enhances creative thinking. One study showed fifty-two students "an awe-inducing 3D-video" and then a neutral one. After each video, the students were administered tests from the Torrance Tests of Creative Thinking. The scientists found a direct causal relationship between awe and creative thinking.[10]

What about belief in the existence of God? In a "spiritually provocative experiment on awe, scientists randomly assigned study participants" to a variety of viewing experiences. The first was a five-minute video of "grand, sweeping shots of plains, mountains, space, and canyons." Another group watched a humorous video, and yet another watched a Mike Wallace interview. After the viewings, those participants who watched the nature video expressed a greater belief in the supernatural as well as a stronger belief in God generally than the other two groups.[11]

Other research has explored what makes church services contribute to the well-being of those who attend. Positive emotions have been identified as the mediating factor, in particular, the positive feeling of self-transcendence, or—you guessed it—awe. But there's a fascinating twist in this research that shows that not all positive emotions contribute to well-being. "Distinguishing between more and less relevant positive emotions in a religious/spiritual context, it was found that the effect was mediated by self-transcendent positive emotions (awe, gratitude, love, and peace) but not by other positive emotions (amusement and pride)."[12] Self-transcendent positive emotions experienced in church contribute to one's well-being, but amusement and pride don't. In other words, the benefit of church life comes through adoration of our holy and majestic King, not from entertainment or from the pride that sometimes attends religion. Gut-splitting laughter or holier-than-thou pomp and ceremony may feel good in the moment, but losing ourselves in God brings lasting satisfaction.

To find ways to incorporate awe into your daily life, check out the "Everyday Awe Finder" in the toolbox.

I'm awestruck by that.

The awesome effects of awe

1. Increase in cooperativeness
2. More sharing
3. Greater sense of community
4. More self-sacrifice
5. More humility
6. Less self-righteousness
7. More belief in God
8. More creativity
9. Better well-being

The "what" of worship

Consider not just the experience of awe but the *object* of awe. Could being awestruck by something powerful but nonbenevolent affect us differently than our awe of God, who is both powerful and benevolent? This seems to be the very point of much of the Bible. Awe is a core component of worship, and what we worship molds who we become. The entire story of God involves a war between Him and His usurpers, contending for the throne of our hearts. It matters not just *that* we worship but *what* we worship.

In the long run, we become like what we worship. In the Bible, the pagans became more like Baal, the Philistines became more like Dagon, and Jesus' worshipers became more like Jesus. This still holds true today. Rex Whitmire Harbour, a man who shot at cars on Highway 365 near Atlanta and then killed himself, was obsessed with the Parkland, Florida, school shooter Nikolas Cruz, saying he was a " 'hero' who gave him 'courage and confidence.' "[13]

Author Kevin Quirk addresses sports addiction in his book *Not Now, Honey, I'm Watching the Game.*[14] The title says it all—the awe of one's sports heroes contributes to addiction, and addiction of any kind can become a relationship-displacing obsession. Dr. Lynn McCutcheon coined the term *celebrity worship syndrome* when she noticed celebrity worship affecting people's lives, making them more prone to "anxiety, depression, high stress levels, poor body image, isolation, and obsessive-compulsive behaviors." Psychologists believe as many as 36 percent of people qualify for celebrity worship syndrome, with our omnipresent screens helping celebrities come into our lives.[15] It's not hard to conceptualize the crushing effect of celebrity idolatry; it's a one-way relationship with people pouring out adoration on "gods" that can never love them back.

Worship in head and heart

If a generic experience of awe can make people more altruistic, wouldn't a more thoughtful, developed sense of awe, one that engages the entire person—body, mind, and heart—have an even more marked effect? If being in awe of trees can make us more inclined to help someone pick up dropped pens, couldn't being in awe of the self-giving Jesus cause us to change "from glory to glory" (2 Corinthians 3:18)? God says, "Stand in awe, and sin not" (Psalm 4:4, KJV).

God calls us to intelligent awe and intelligent worship. Observe what happened with the Samaritan woman whom Jesus met at the well in Sychar (John 4). Awe built upon awe throughout the encounter. The Jews hated the Samaritans, but Jesus asked this Samaritan woman for water, which was the first surprise. He then held a civil conversation with her—surprise number two. He revealed that He knew her immoral past and present, which was the third surprise. She was sweating already, but when Jesus delivered surprise number four by telling her He was the Messiah, her adrenaline shot to the max. She abandoned her waterpot to run through town on the most spontaneous evangelistic campaign of all time. Wave after wave of shock and awe gave her a surge of energy; the kindness and respect of this holy Jew and the evidence He gave of His divinity gave her a message.

In the midst of the conversation, Jesus said something intriguing about worship: "God is Spirit, and those who worship Him must worship in spirit and truth" (verse 24). What does it mean to "worship in spirit and truth"? Jesus had just finished telling this other-side-of-the-tracks woman that Jews "know what we worship, for salvation is of the Jews" (verse 22). He referred to "the oracles of God," the Holy Scriptures, which are the written, cognitively detailed expression of God's plan for humanity committed to the Jews (Romans 3:2). True worship, Jesus said, embraced specific truth about God.

True worship engages the head and heart. Much of what passes as worship in churches today involves overwhelming the emotions but checking the mind at the door or, in another imbalance, a dry formalism that leaves the heart untouched. True worship involves engagement of the cerebral cortex with profound themes and timeless truths about the self-giving love of God that, through the Holy Spirit, flow down into the deepest chambers of the heart because they speak to the most significant issues of the heart. That revelation of love then ascends back to God in praise and adoration. This is what Jesus meant by worshiping in Spirit and truth.

Worship wars

The world will one day divide over two distinct types of awe: the awe of God, or the awe of His enemy. In the book of Revelation, we see world history come to a close in a global conflict symbolized through various beasts. The nefarious sea beast colludes with the earth beast to form a religious-political conglomerate that uses economic boycotts and an imposed death penalty to force the masses into submission. And "all the world marveled and followed the beast" in awe of its power, but to what end (Revelation 13:3)? So it could blaspheme, persecute, and coerce. Awe indeed disarms us, blowing away our defenses and opening our minds to larger realities. This can be used for evil as well as good, and the beasts of the world know that.

Revelation's story continues with three messages given by angels. The messages command us to worship God and warn against the worship of the beast. The entire world splits into God worshipers and beast worshipers, and the end comes. The God worshipers continue to worship God for eternity, and the beast worshipers come to an end in the lake of fire. Clearly, who or what we worship has serious implications!

Fear God

The first angel in Revelation 14 says, "Fear God and give glory to Him, for the hour of His judgment has come; and worship Him who made heaven and earth, the sea and springs of water" (verse 7). Fear God? As in, be *afraid* of? Or is it to be in *awe* of Him? Or both?

Fear accompanies awe; a tidal wave, a giant animal, or a towering height would all provoke both. The biblical word most often translated as "fear" is *phobos,* similar to *phobia. Phobos* simply indicates the nervous system's arousal in the face of something powerful and potentially dangerous. We are told more than three hundred times to "fear God," meaning to experience awe in the face of His utter power and majesty. The initial fear we feel before a holy and powerful God is, according to the wise man, "the beginning of wisdom" (Proverbs 9:10). At some point in our life's journey, God pulls our attention away from all the idols, points to Himself, and says, "I am more powerful than any of them!"

He doesn't stop there. He captures our attention in order to facilitate a focus on the full truth about Him. As you observe God and are in awe of His power, another of His qualities emerges. Gradually, He conveys His core, self-defining trait—the trait that encompasses all others and from which He never departs. It appears in soft yet majestic hues and layers of dignified grace; it is fierce, fiery, yet quintessentially kind.

It is *love.*

"Perfect love casts out fear" and that displacing love flows back to Him in worship and adoration (1 John 4:18).

As morally sensate beings, using our worship capacity in harmony with our design means that we worship the One who made us and loves us:

"You are worthy, O Lord,
To receive glory and honor and power;
For You created all things,
And by Your will they exist and were created" (Revelation 4:11).

When the Creator became the Redeemer and sacrificed Himself on our behalf, He gave us yet another reason to worship Him. "Worthy is the Lamb who was slain to receive power and riches and wisdom, and strength and honor and glory and blessing!" (Revelation 5:12).

We worship God because He made and redeemed us, loving us at every step.

The masses worship the beast figure of Revelation because of its power alone, but the followers of the Lamb worship God because of His love. The worship controversy in

Revelation is over the love of power versus the power of love. Will we direct our awe mechanism toward a usurper who seduces us with signs and wonders and then forces us to his feet out of megalomaniacal dominance, or will we direct our awe mechanism back to the One who gave us the gift of awe in the first place?

For some guidance on Sabbath keeping, see "Sabbath Joy" in the toolbox.

True worship is a worship borne of love. We can experience worship formed and guided by a knowledge of the truth of God and enlivened by the Spirit of God.

God was so committed to giving us this experience that He set aside an entire twenty-four-hour period each week to part from the mundane facets of life and soak up the spiritual aspects. He was so sure we would feel guilty about taking that much time off that He made it a commandment:

"Remember the Sabbath day by keeping it holy. Six days you shall labor and do all your work, but the seventh day is a sabbath to the LORD your God. On it you shall not do any work, neither you, nor your son or daughter, nor your male or female servant, nor your animals, nor any foreigner residing in your towns. For in six days the LORD made the heavens and the earth, the sea, and all that is in them, but he rested on the seventh day. Therefore the LORD blessed the Sabbath day and made it holy" (Exodus 20:8–11, NIV).

"Had the Sabbath been universally kept, man's thoughts and affections would have been led to the Creator as the object of reverence and worship, and there would never have been an idolater, an atheist, or an infidel."[16]

Dacher Keltner says, "Awe motivates attachment to leaders and principles that transcend the self."[17] Our awe of God serves to attach us to Him who transcends us.

"Stand in awe of Him" (Psalm 33:8).

DISCUSSION QUESTIONS

1. Share a time when God worked miraculously in your life.

2. Share some everyday experiences that provoke a sense of awe.

3. If you had to choose between a life full of big miracles and a life of everyday miracles, which would you choose? Why?

4. Scientific research can show us the benefit of awe, but not who is worthy of our worship. Have you ever worshiped something unworthy of worship? How did things turn out?

5. Celebrity worship is correlated with many negative effects. What causes these negative effects?

6. Describe a time when you experienced true worship.

7. Share how a healthy fear of God served a purpose in your life and growth.

8. Do you remember a time in your life when perfect love cast out fear? Explain.

9. What are some of your favorite memories of being in awe of God and worshiping Him?

10. What do you think heaven will be like?

1. Heather Thompson Day, *Confessions of a Christian Wife* (Nampa, ID: Pacific Press®, 2018), 45–47.

2. *Webster's Third New International Dictionary*, Unabridged ed., s.v. "awe," accessed June 19, 2019, http://unabridged .merriam-webster.com/unabridged/awe.

3. Matthew Hutson, "Awesomeness Is Everything," *Atlantic*, February 15, 2017, https://www.theatlantic.com/magazine /archive/2017/01/awesomeness-is-everything/508775/.

4. Albert Einstein, "Albert Einstein," in *Living Philosophies* (New York: Simon and Schuster, 1931), 6.

5. Dacher Keltner, "Why Do We Feel Awe?" *Greater Good Magazine*, May 10, 2016, https://greatergood.berkeley.edu/article /item/why_do_we_feel_awe.

6. Keltner, "Why Do We Feel Awe?"

7. Paul Piff and Dacher Keltner, "Why Do We Experience Awe?" Opinion, *New York Times*, May 22, 2015, https://www .nytimes.com/2015/05/24/opinion/sunday/why-do-we-experience-awe.html.

8. Michelle N. Shiota, Dacher Keltner, and Amanda Mossman, "The Nature of Awe: Elicitors, Appraisals, and Effects on Self-Concept," *Cognition and Emotion* 21, no. 5 (2007): 944–963, https://doi.org/10.1080/02699930600923668.

9. Keltner, "Why Do We Feel Awe?"

10. Alice Chirico et. al., "Awe Enhances Creative Thinking: An Experimental Study," *Creativity Research Journal* 30, no. 2 (2018): 123–131, https://doi.org/10.1080/10400419.2018.1446491.

11. Andy Tix, "Awe in Religious and Spiritual Experience," *Psychology Today*, November 7, 2017, https://www .psychologytoday.com/us/blog/the-pursuit-peace/201711/awe-in-religious-and-spiritual-experience.

12. Patty Van Cappellen et al., "Religion and Well-Being: The Mediating Role of Positive Emotions," *Journal of Happiness Studies* 17, no. 2 (April 2016): 485–505, https://link.springer.com/article/10.1007/s10902-014-9605-5.

13. Crimesider staff, "Sheriff: Highway Sniper's Writings Show He 'Idolized' Parkland Shooter Nikolas Cruz," *CBS News*, May 7, 2018, https://www.cbsnews.com/news/sheriff-highway-sniper-who-wounded-two-in-ga-idolized-parkland-school-shooter/.

14. Kevin Quirk, *Not Now, Honey, I'm Watching the Game* (New York: Fireside, 1997).

15. Samantha Olson, "The Psychological Effects of Idolatry: How Celebrity Crushes Impact Children's Health," Medical Daily, October 25, 2015, https://www.medicaldaily.com/psychological-effects-idolatry-how-celebrity-crushes-impact-childrens -health-358604.

16. Ellen G. White, *The Great Controversy* (Mountain View, CA: Pacific Press®, 1911), 438.

17. "Dacher Keltner," Department of Psychology, University of California, Berkeley, accessed June 19, 2019, https://psychology.berkeley.edu/people/dacher-keltner.

This tool works best with a sit-down conversation between two or more people with a significant conflict.[1] It is the most effective in one of three situations:

1. The people in conflict are experienced in using this tool.
2. The people in conflict aren't experienced with this tool, but they have a capable mediator or coach to help structure the conversation.
3. One of the people in the conflict has a high level of maturity and is willing to set the tone and take the initiative in this process.

To remember the five steps, we use the vowels A, E, I, O, and U. Flip a coin or play rock-paper-scissors to identify the person who will start by telling his or her side of the issue, then do the following:

1. *Agree*. Find the truth in what the other person is saying. Your narratives won't line up totally, but neither will they be completely dissimilar. Identify what you *can* agree with.
2. *Empathize*. Put yourself in the other person's place. If you experienced things as this individual did, how would you feel? Remember, you don't need to agree; you simply need to understand and convey that understanding in your words and tone. The best way to convey empathy is to state the other person's viewpoint in your own words and then express your own feelings of empathy in response.
3. *Inquire*. Ask the person whether you understand his or her view correctly and whether he or she wants to add or change anything. Draw the individual out with more questions, approaching him or her with curiosity rather than defensiveness. Eventually, inquire as to whether he or she feels understood or not. The idea is that the first three steps will help the person feel understood to the point that he or she can hear the other person's view.
4. *Open up*. Tell the person that you would now like to share your view. With the individual's cooperation (and most of the time, the person will cooperate), express your viewpoint. Begin by affirming the positives, such as your appreciation of the person and your faith that things will get better. Then cautiously share the negative aspects.
5. *Uplift*. Express your appreciation of the person, and find a way to uplift him or her. Affirm the relationship and restate your love and commitment. Lift up the person and your relationship in prayer.

Here's how conflict typically goes without radical resolution:

It's Jennifer's birthday, and Elise promised her that they would spend the day together. They meet at a coffee shop and spend some time visiting, but then Elise seems to be absorbed in her phone. Jennifer starts to feel hurt because Elise seems distracted. What Jennifer doesn't know is that Elise is texting a group of Jennifer's friends about a surprise birthday party they are planning for that evening. Elise tries to stay involved in the conversation, but the texts are urgent. She is trying to finalize the plan for the cake.

Jennifer grows more and more frustrated and hurt until she explodes: "I feel like you are not even paying attention to me! It's really rude. I mean, it's my *birthday*, and you told me we were going to spend the day together. I don't want to spend the day watching you on your phone!"

Elise responds, "You are really overreacting, Jennifer. I am texting about something really important. How do you know I am not doing something for you?"

"Something for me? Why would I assume that when you clearly don't care about me or want to hang out with me?"

"Maybe I would want to hang out with you more if you didn't attack me like this!"

And so on, down the spiral.

Now let's see how it goes when we use the AEIOU tool:

Jennifer says, "I feel like you are not even paying attention to me! It's really rude. I mean, it's my *birthday*, and you told me we were going to spend the day together. I don't want to spend the day watching you on your phone!"

Elise says, "Oh, well, yeah. I can see how you would feel that way. I am on my phone a lot. I did say we would be hanging out today (*agree*). I don't like it either when people stare at their phones rather than talk to me (*empathize*). I wonder, Does this happen a lot with me? Do you feel like I am distracted and focused on my devices (*inquire*)?"

Jennifer, already calming down, says, "Well, yes. I am not as tech savvy as you, and I feel a little lost when we are together and you connect elsewhere."

Jennifer has just given Elise some good information about her insecurities.

Elise continues her inquiries: "Do you feel a little more sensitive on your birthday too? I know I do, even though I hate to admit it."

Jennifer says, "Yeah, I was raised by parents who didn't believe in celebrating birthdays, and I always felt left out of 'normal' society." Bingo! Jennifer has just opened up a whole world of pain that Elise unintentionally triggered.

Elise continues to empathize and inquire, and Jennifer continues to calm down and feel understood.

Finally, Elise says, "Hey, do you mind if I share something with you about why it seemed as if I was being rude by being on my phone?"

Jennifer agrees.

Elise says, "I was finalizing plans for your cake. We are throwing a surprise party for you. We will be going out to eat together, then going back to my house for cake."

Right then, a bunch of Jennifer's friends walk into the coffee shop. And they all live happily ever after.

Not everything will turn out as perfectly as this little vignette, but this tool really does have the power to settle a conflict, successfully address root issues, and strengthen the sense of safety in the relationship.

---

1. This tool was created by Elise Harboldt, who adapted it from David Burns, *Feeling Good Together* (New York: Broadway Books, 2008).

THE "BIG FIVE" PERSONALITY TRAITS

The five-factor model of personality (FFM) is used to understand the relationship between personality traits and learning.[1] It uses the acronym OCEAN:

- *Openness* to experience involves curiosity and a preference for novelty and variety. People with high levels of openness may be more prone to experimentation with substances but also the arts. They tend to seek out euphoric experiences, whereas people with low openness may seek fulfillment through perseverance and discipline.
- *Conscientiousness* reflects the trait of being organized, dependable, disciplined, and preferring to plan rather than being spontaneous. Low conscientiousness can be perceived as inconsistency, lack of reliability, and sloppiness.
- *Extraversion* involves energy, assertiveness, and sociability. People who rate high in extraversion can be perceived as attention seeking, domineering; those who rank low may be perceived as aloof.
- *Agreeableness* is the tendency to be sensitive and cooperative rather than suspicious and antagonistic. Agreeable people trust and help others, sometimes to the point of naivety or lacking assertiveness. People with low levels of agreeableness can be competitive and difficult to get along with.
- *Neuroticism* means having greater difficulty coping with psychological stress and an inclination toward negative emotions. People who rank low in neuroticism can seem uninspiring and unconcerned; highly neurotic people are more reactive and excitable.

I am the life of the party. E					
I feel much concern for others. A					
I am always prepared. C					
I get stressed out easily. N					
I have a rich vocabulary. O					
I talk a lot. E					
I am interested in people. A					
I don't leave my belongings around. C					
I am tense most of the time. N					
I find it easy to understand abstract ideas. O					
I feel comfortable around people. E					

	Disagree (0)	Disagree somewhat (1)	Neutral (2)	Agree Somewhat (3)	Agree (4)
I never insult people. A					
I pay attention to details. C					
I worry about things. N					
I have a vivid imagination. O					
I don't stay in the background. E					
I sympathize with others' feelings. A					
I keep things clean. C					
I tend to feel blue. N					
I find abstract ideas very interesting. O					
I start conversations. E					
I am interested in other people's problems. A					
I get chores done right away. C					
I am easily disturbed. N					
I have excellent ideas. O					
I have a lot to say. E					
I have a soft heart. A					
I put things back in their proper place. C					
I don't get upset easily. N					
I have a good imagination. O					
I talk to a lot of different people at parties. O					
I am really interested in others. A					
I like order. C					
I change my mood a lot. N					
I am quick to understand things. O					
I like to draw attention to myself. E					
I take time out for others. A					

THE "BIG FIVE" PERSONALITY TRAITS (cont.)

	Disagree (0)	Disagree somewhat (1)	Neutral (2)	Agree Somewhat (3)	Agree (4)
I don't shirk my duties. C					
I have frequent mood swings. N					
I use difficult words. O					
I don't mind being the center of attention. E					
I feel others' emotions. A					
I follow a schedule. C					
I get irritated easily. N					
I spend little time reflecting on things. E					
I am comfortable around strangers. E					
I make people feel at ease. A					
I am exacting in my work. C					
I often feel stressed. N					
I am full of ideas. O					

Each trait has ten descriptions. Add up your points for each description, with a maximum of forty points per trait. Compare your numbers, and see which traits rank the highest.

Disagree: 0 points
Somewhat disagree: 1 point
Neutral: 2 points
Somewhat agree: 3 points
Agree: 4 points

---

1. This tool has been adapted from the "Big Five Personality Test" at the Open-Source Psychometrics Project (https://openpsychometrics.org/tests/IPIP-BFFM/). This free test is available online, and it will create a graphic from your results.

Understanding and communicating our own emotions effectively is one of the most important skills involved in intimate relationships. We all start to feel disconnected from our loved ones at times. Use this little exercise to help regain a sense of connection.

Because this type of exercise encourages vulnerability, this tool generally is not recommended for relationships in which there is any kind of abuse—physical, emotional, verbal, financial, or religious. Abusive individuals will exploit vulnerability. If you are in an abusive relationship, seek professional help or call the National Domestic Violence Hotline at 1-800-799-SAFE.

1. *Approach* your loved one with a request to do a relationship-building exercise. (You can mention that you found it in a book you are reading, and you would like to try it out.) It can take from ten minutes to an hour.

2. *Agree* together to follow the method and the basic purpose of the method:
   a. To understand one another
   b. To become aware of and acknowledge the emotions in the relationship
   c. To increase emotional security in the relationship

3. *Pray* together for help to avoid defensiveness and to keep true to the purpose of the exercise.

4. *Touch* one another in some way, such as handholding or sitting face to face.

5. *Gaze* into each other's eyes as you speak.

6. *Ask* the following questions, *one person at a time*:
   a. Do you feel connected to me?
   b. What things do I do that help you to feel connected to me?
   c. What things do I do that keep you from feeling connected to me?
   d. How can I improve your sense of connection to me?

7. *Summarize* what the other person said after each answer.

8. *Switch* to the other person asking the same series of questions, with that person summarizing the other's answers.

9. *Hug* for six seconds. Research shows longer hugs stir up bonding chemicals.

10. *Repeat* every day for a month, and then see if you would like to make this exercise a permanent part of your life.

How does divine emotion compare with human emotion? Recognizing the commonalities can help us to feel more connected to an emotional God.

Look up the Bible passage, identify the emotion, and give an example of when you felt the same emotion.

Passage	When have I felt the same?
Genesis 6:6	
Exodus 20:5	
Judges 2:18	
Isaiah 62:5	
Isaiah 63:10	
Jeremiah 31:3	
Zephaniah 3:17	
Psalm 11:5	
Psalm 103:13	
Psalm 106:40	
Proverbs 6:16–19	
Matthew 20:34	
Matthew 23:37–39	
Mark 10:21	
Matthew 27:46	
John 11:33–35	
Revelation 3:16	

After each entry, rate your level of participation from zero to ten (ten being the most). Consider writing down an example from your own experience on a separate piece of paper or in a journal.[1]

Blaming: You project personal responsibility on to other people or circumstances. "If he had been kinder, I wouldn't have cheated. He made me do it!" _____

Catastrophizing: You think that past, present, and/or future events will be awful and unbearable. "If I don't get an A, it will be horrible!" _____

Dichotomous thinking: You regard situations and people in all-or-nothing, black-and-white terms. "Either we have fun on this camp-out, or we don't!" _____

Discounting positives: You trivialize the positive things you and others do. "Of course, I take care of my children. Who wouldn't?" _____

Emotional reasoning: You believe that because you feel something, it must be so. "I am feeling guilty. I must be guilty!" _____

External locus of control: You believe that life "happens" to you, and you minimize the effect your choices have on the outcome. "I can't be happy unless so-and-so changes. It's totally in this person's hands." _____

Fallacy of fairness: You believe that everything must be measured on the basis of fairness and equality, and you fail to accept the reality that things aren't always that way. "He cheated, so now I will cheat." _____

Fortune-telling: You assume the past is entirely predictive of the future, rather than allowing for change. "I failed in that relationship, so I must not have what it takes." _____

Judgment focus: You view events, situations, or people completely in terms of how they measure against some arbitrary standard, rather than just seeing things for what they are. "He's too talkative, and people don't like him because of it." _____

Labeling: This is a severe type of overgeneralization involving the practice of labeling a person or other entity after having little exposure. "That day care center is child-abuse central." _____

Mind-reading: Without evidence, you assume that your intuitions never misfire and that you know what people are thinking about things. "I can tell they hated my lecture." _____

Monsterifying: You exaggerate the wrongs of others, attributing to them a global pattern of evil for which you lack evidence. "She is wholly given over to evil and can't be trusted." _____

Negative filtering: You perceive only the worst of past and present events and circumstances. "Everyone I have ever known has rejected me." _____

Overgeneralizing: You apply negative traits or actions to the entire person or situation. "My husband can't do anything right!" _____

DISTORTED THOUGHTS (cont.)

Overidentifying: You see yourself entirely in terms of one trait or event. "My shyness makes me into a complete, antisocial reject." _____

Overvaluing: You attribute to others excessive authority or worth in contrast with yourself and/or others. "She always knows what's best for me. She is never wrong! I can't take a step without her." _____

Personalizing: You take an undue amount of responsibility upon yourself. "If I looked better, my husband wouldn't be into pornography." _____

Projecting: You see others through the lens of your own traits, assuming they share them. "Of course, he was angry! I _would_ be angry!" _____

Regret orientation: You focus on past mishaps, assuming that they have been ruinous to your life. "If only I hadn't gotten that surgery!" _____

Self-inflation: You claim personal assets, achievements, and abilities while lacking the courage to test your beliefs. "I am a great singer. If I tried, I could be famous." _____

Self-serving bias: You see all positive events as due to your goodness, and all negative events as outside your control. "People hate me because they are hateful, but when they love me, it's because I'm so awesome." _____

Shoulds: You see people and events entirely in terms of ideals rather than reality. "People should be friendly and warm." _____

Singling: You place yourself in positions of complete contrast to others. "God's forgiveness is for everyone, but I am too evil." _____

Supernaturalizing: You interpret events and circumstances too readily and confidently in terms of direct divine intervention. "People don't like me, so God must be judging me." _____

Unfair comparisons: You view yourself in contrast to unrealistic standards. "If I am not as smart as he is, I won't even try." _____

---

1. Some of the concepts in this tool were adapted from R. L. Leahy and S. J. Holland, *Treatment Plans and Interventions for Depression and Anxiety Disorders* (New York: Guilford Press, 2000), 299.

Empathy, with its sense of connectedness and shared experience, forms a basis for good communication. This exercise will help us to learn the skills of developing effective, empathic bonds with one another. Often when this empathy develops in a relationship, the problems seem to solve themselves.

Meditation: Our inclination in relationships tends toward selfishness. We want to be heard and to advance our own agendas. But empathy requires excellent listening.

- "So then, my beloved brethren, let every man be swift to hear, slow to speak, slow to wrath" (James 1:19).
- "In the multitude of words sin is not lacking, but he who restrains his lips is wise" (Proverbs 10:19).
- "He who answers a matter before he hears it, it is folly and shame to him" (Proverbs 18:13).

Notice the advice in James 1:19. He invites us to learn to be (1) "swift to hear," (2) "slow to speak," and (3) "slow to wrath."

Unfortunately, most of the time, we respond in the opposite way. We are typically (1) *slow* to hear, (2) *swift* to speak, and (3) *swift* to wrath.

Following the counsel of James takes us in the opposite direction of our inclinations. This exercise will help us to learn this new way of doing things.

Remember this equation: Empathy = Ask and Reflect.

Two essential components to empathic listening are *asking* questions and *reflecting* what we hear.

1. *Asking questions.* The purpose of asking questions is to draw out the thoughts, feelings, and opinions of the other. Try to use What, Where, When, and How questions. Try to avoid asking Why questions because these questions can often sound accusatory. Make sure the questions aren't veiled accusations, as in, "What makes you act so mean all the time?"
2. *Reflecting.* The purpose of reflection is likewise to draw the person out. The point of reflecting is not to agree or disagree with the person but to understand him or her. Simply put in your own words what you heard the other person say, asking him or her to confirm or correct. Again, the point is to understand. You are not going for the objective truth but their subjective truth.

Meditation: As the expression goes, "People don't care how much you know until they know how much you care." Remember that the point of empathy is not to *agree* with people but to *understand* them. Once they sense that you have joined them in their subjective world, they will often begin to trust you. After their trust is in place, you will be able to correct their misconceptions.

Remember that you might be the one in error too. "Brethren, if a man is overtaken in any trespass, you who are spiritual restore such a one in a spirit of gentleness, considering yourself lest you also be tempted. Bear one another's burdens, and so fulfill the law of Christ. For if anyone thinks himself to be something, when he is nothing, he deceives himself" (Galatians 6:1–3). Establishing empathy creates an environment that encourages taking responsibility.

Awe is available if we only take the time to experience it. Here are some simple ways to experience awe:

- Look up at a tall tree for a full minute.
- Gaze at the stars for a full minute.
- Take a walk in your neighborhood, noticing everything as if for the first time.
- Watch a sunrise or sunset.
- Listen to classical music, such as Handel's *Messiah* or hymns sung by large choirs.
- Spend time with and enter into the experience of a child. Children are always in awe!
- Look into a loved one's eyes for a full minute.
- Notice a fabulous aroma, such as baking bread or lavender.
- Experience a storm.
- Walk on a beach with big waves.
- Climb a mountain.
- Read a Bible chapter, such as Psalm 23, John 3, or 1 Corinthians 13.
- Do a topical Bible study.
- Read miracle stories from such publications as *Guideposts*.
- Be part of a large crowd at an event.
- Study science, learning about such things as the miracle of conception.
- Think about the fact that God has no beginning.
- Meditate on the vastness of the ocean.
- Consider the stars and that space goes on for infinity.
- Believe that God loves you just as you are and always will.
- Study the deep, mind-expanding themes of the Bible, such as atonement.

This exercise is designed to assist in thought control, which helps stabilize mood and emotions. I have broken this process down into three main steps: find, argue, and replace, or FAR.

Find

First, find or identify the triggering event or circumstance: "My boss ignores me." "There was a traffic jam."

Now, learn to identify your anxious or sad feelings and admit to yourself that you are feeling them. Use the "Feeling Tree" worksheet in the toolbox.

Next, find the thoughts that underlie the feelings. Here are some examples of thoughts that underlie feelings: "I will miss this deadline, lose my job, and live in poverty." "That person thinks he is better than me. I hate to be put down!" This will take more time and energy, even prayer, because often these thoughts are unconscious or nearly so. Write the thoughts in the space provided on the next page.

Congratulations, you have accomplished the first step!

Argue

Learn to argue with yourself. Use the "Distorted Thoughts" worksheet in the toolbox. In doing this, you are breaking up the fallow ground of your own thinking so that the seed of truth can take root. Tell yourself what's wrong with the way you are thinking: "I'm catastrophizing missing the deadline. I am making it much worse than it is!" Or, "Where is the evidence that person thinks he is better than me? I am mind reading. And I am also catastrophizing how bad it is to deal with an arrogant person." In this step, you are not beating yourself up; you are holding yourself accountable for the way you are thinking and treating yourself.

Replace

Learn to replace misbeliefs with truth. Truth will be much more nuanced, complex, and detailed than distorted thinking. If the distorted thought is, *My wife is an idiot, and I can't stand it!* then the truth would be something like, *My wife gets distracted sometimes when too much is going on. She loses her concentration. Sometimes she makes mistakes—locking the keys in the car or leaving the stove on all night. Most of the time, the mistakes aren't catastrophic. A few times they have caused inconvenience. But she has a PhD in microbiology, so it's not that she lacks intelligence. I get frustrated with her, but her occasional flakiness isn't horrible; it's just irritating.* Truth has shades of gray, whereas distorted thinking tends to be very black and white or extreme.

Use the following table to write your answers.

Find	Argue	Replace
Event: Feeling word: Thought:		
Event: Feeling word: Thought:		
Event: Feeling word: Thought:		
Event: Feeling word: Thought:		
Event: Feeling word: Thought:		
Event: Feeling word: Thought:		
Event: Feeling word: Thought:		
Event: Feeling word: Thought:		
Event: Feeling word: Thought:		
Event: Feeling word: Thought:		
Event: Feeling word: Thought:		
Event: Feeling word: Thought:		

FEELING TREE

Start on the ground, look up at the tree, and see the primary emotions on the first branches. Ask yourself which of those you are experiencing. Follow the primary emotion to the secondary emotions to refine further what you are feeling, then move on to the tertiary emotions. Write down all the emotions that apply.

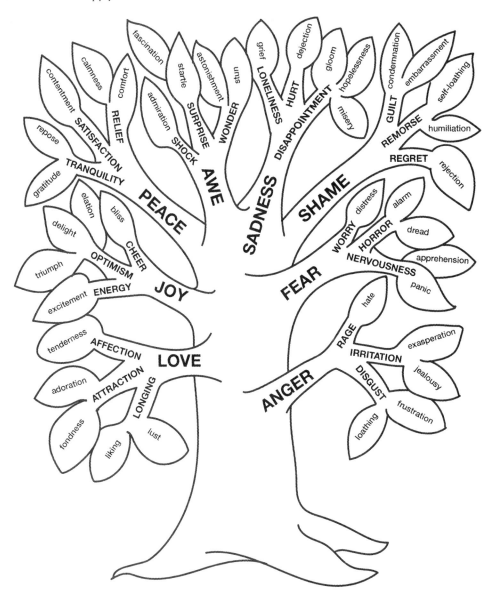

Ask yourself what life experiences and circumstances have molded your core beliefs. The lies we believe come in four primary areas:

1. Lies about ourselves
2. Lies about other people
3. Lies about the future
4. Lies about God

One good way to find out what your core beliefs are is to ask other people. I recommend choosing two or three people and asking them these questions:

1. What do you think I believe about myself?
2. What do you think I believe about other people?
3. What do you think I believe about the future?
4. What do you think I believe about God?

Next, do some journaling. I recommend using the narrative approach, telling your story in kind of a storybook fashion: "Once there was a little girl who grew up in a home with a nice mom and dad and, eventually, a cute baby brother. She thought the world was a warm, friendly place. Then she met a bully on the way to school one day . . ." An alternative to a written narrative is an artistic time line. Draw a horizontal line on a large piece of paper, marking off the major events as they occurred and illustrating them with paints, crayons, or another medium.

I also recommend taking a walk to contemplate these questions. Pray while walking, and ask God to show you what your core beliefs are.

Take all that you learn from dialoguing with others, your journaling or art, and your prayer walk, and distill these thoughts down into your core belief system on yourself, other people, God, and the future.

Now you can start to correct those core beliefs, replacing them with truth. Write affirmations on index cards and carry them with you, reading them throughout the day when your stress levels rise. Share what you learned through this process with other people too.

TOOLBOX

Use the "Floor Technique" to utilize the skills in "Establishing Empathy With EAR." Flip a coin. The winner goes first. This person gets "the floor" (you can use a rug or a tile or simply use a book or other object). While this person has the floor, the other must use the EAR technique to draw out the first person's view, feelings, and thoughts.

Here is a sample of what *not* to do:

FRED. (Who has the floor.) I feel lonely at times in our relationship—as if you have withdrawn from me.

SARAH. I have only withdrawn because you are so pushy and demanding!

Notice that Sarah advanced her own agenda and talked from her own subjective experience, rather than drawing out Fred's subjective experience.

Here is a sample of what *to* do:

FRED. I feel lonely at times in our relationship—as if you have withdrawn from me.

SARAH. How long have you felt this way? (*Asking*)

FRED. Just since the baby was born. I feel like he took my place in your heart.

SARAH. So you feel kind of displaced by Tommy. (*Reflecting*)

FRED. Yeah. My parents never paid much attention to me growing up, and I feel like it's happening all over again.

SARAH. Let me see if I understand you: my paying so much attention to Tommy reminds you of your childhood? (*Asking and reflecting*)

FRED. Yeah.

SARAH. Was there a "Tommy" in your family? Someone who got all the attention?

FRED. Yeah, my little brother, Frank. He was my parents' favorite. They said so.

SARAH. It must have been really hard to have your parents play favorites.

FRED. I felt so rejected.

Notice how quickly this conversation arrived at the root of the problem—Fred's fear of rejection. Sarah's effective asking and listening got to the root of the problem. Fred felt understood and heard. From this point on, the couple could work out some simple solutions to prevent Fred's fear of rejection. Simply being heard and understood by his wife probably accomplished this as much as any follow-up steps.

People don't care how much you know until they know how much you care. Remember that the point of empathy is not to *agree* with people but to *understand* them. Once they sense that you have joined them in their subjective world, they will often begin to trust you. After their trust is in place, you will be able to correct their misconceptions.

Remember that you might be the one in error too. Establishing empathy creates an environment that encourages taking responsibility.

Be aware that empathy exercises shouldn't be used with abusive or highly manipulative individuals. Most marriage counselors don't even facilitate joint marriage-counseling sessions if one of the spouses is abusive because the abusive or manipulative individual will be inclined to take advantage of "soft" emotions.

This worksheet was designed to help those of us who recognize our need to forgive.

Failure to forgive results in bitterness. According to Hebrews 12:15, bitterness has several features: it constitutes a failure to be filled with grace; it is a root and, therefore, deep within us; it springs up and causes trouble; and it defiles many. Considering its high cost to our well-being and the well-being of others, we would do well to forgive. Yet forgiveness seems difficult.

I try to approach the issue with biblical integrity and compassion. It is my intention and prayer that through meditation and the following action steps, you will be led to a decision forgive, which will help in your healing process.

Action Step: I encourage you to take a day off while working through this sheet. Go somewhere, preferably surrounded by nature, where you can be alone and quiet. If you are inside, light some candles and put on gentle music. Don't bring your laptop, but bring a Bible, a hymnal, and your personal calendar. You may want to fast or semifast on fruit or fruit and bread. The point is to reduce distractions and focus on the task. This is a life-and-death issue.

Meditation: Jesus taught us to pray like this: "Forgive us our debts, as we also have forgiven our debtors" (Matthew 6:12, NIV). The word *as* is the Greek *hós*, which can mean "as," "like as," "even as," or "when." Essentially, *hós* joints two parts: God's forgiveness of our sin and our forgiveness of others' sin. The two link together like sunshine and birdsong, rain and verdure. Likewise, Jesus taught, "And whenever you stand praying, if you have anything against anyone, forgive him, that your Father in heaven may also forgive you your trespasses" (Mark 11:25). Notice the bidirectional grace—receiving from God and giving to others.

We needn't wait for people who have wronged us to repent before forgiving them. We might wait forever! In the above examples, we are commanded to forgive any and all "debtors" and "anyone" we have anything against. This forgiveness must be settled between our souls and God before we can hope for it to trickle down into the human realm.

Think of forgiveness in terms of water. God pours forgiveness into our vessels, washing away our sin and filling us with grace. We then spill out water on our thirsty, dirty fellow travelers. We share the forgiveness we receive from God. But if we hold our vessels tight to our chests, refusing to forgive others, God won't be able to fill our vessels. *Bestowing forgiveness expands our capacity to receive God's forgiveness.* Likewise, receiving forgiveness from God inspires us to forgive others. The giving and receiving of forgiveness exist symbiotically, in mutual sustenance of one another.

But forgiving those who have deeply wronged us presents a serious challenge. Bitter feelings cling like burrs, causing further pain. Forgiveness, *aphiémi* in Greek, means "send away." Sending those bitter feelings away sounds like a good option at times, but at other times, it feels as if this would leave us vulnerable to more hurt.

Wounded people must get distance from their wrongdoers in order to process the pain. Without this distance, forgiveness is much more difficult. Ideally, victims of domestic violence move out; employees of a sexually harassing boss relocate; and adult children of emotionally abusive parents create appropriate boundaries. At times, victims may have difficulty creating physical distance, so emotional distance must suffice.

Action Step: Answer the following question: How can you create appropriate distance from your wrongdoer, if you haven't already?

Meditation: Many people, especially abuse victims, have a confused understanding of forgiveness. Some were trained from a young age to excuse or even approve of abuse. Perpetrators know how to find and push guilt buttons so that victims feel that imposing any accountability for wrong done is un-Christian and unkind. Others have negative feelings or memories and assume that this means they haven't yet forgiven. Distorted ideas of forgiveness prevent true forgiveness. Use this list to rout out false ideas of forgiveness:

- *Forgiveness does not equal trust.* Notice that even the great apostle Paul, who was forgiven by God and by the Christians he persecuted, had to earn the trust of the church (Acts 9). Forgiveness is not trust. Of course, forgiveness is indeed the first step toward the restoration of trust, so trust in some cases grows out of forgiveness.
- *Forgiveness does not equal excusing.* Forgiveness is the opposite of excusing or overlooking sin. Built right into the concept of forgiveness is the acknowledgment that wrong was done. By forgiving, you are making a clear statement that what the individual did was wrong. Through the Cross, God made a forgiveness statement to the world. He proved that sin couldn't be excused, but forgiveness of sin brings restoration.
- *Forgiveness does not equal approval.* To forgive a person in no way indicates approval of the behavior on your part. You may even choose to forgive a person who continues to do wrong, just as Jesus forgave the Roman soldiers who nailed Him to the cross. By forgiving, you are actually showing your *disapproval* of the act.

- *Forgiveness does not equal forgetting.* While putting people's sins out of our minds is one of the benefits of forgiveness (we don't have to think about them anymore!), it is unrealistic and unreasonable to expect that they will be completely forgotten. We must find a delicate balance of admitting things happened without dwelling upon them.
- *Forgiveness does not equal feeling.* Forgiveness is a choice—not a feeling. Often we will wrestle with negative feelings long after we have forgiven. Feelings are not evidence of whether we have forgiven or not. They are just feelings. Feelings are important, but they are not conclusive evidence of reality. Typically, if we choose to forgive and then act in accordance with that choice, negative feelings will abate over time. But if there isn't adequate distance (physical or emotional) between the wrongdoer and the victim, emotional healing will be much more difficult.

Action Step: Read the above list of misconceptions carefully and answer the following questions: Have I cherished any of these distorted ideas of forgiveness? If so, have they prevented me from forgiving? If so, how?

Meditation: Forgiveness is a learned skill—a science and an art. It is a conscientious, rational process of releasing the wrongdoer from the consequences of sin. Many metaphors help us understand it, but Jesus' Magna Carta on forgiveness—Matthew 18—uses debt, debt collecting, and debt forgiveness to illustrate.

In this chapter, Jesus first addresses the offender by warning against stumbling blocks—wrongs done that cause "little ones" to "stumble" (verse 6). Jesus gives very clear and shocking warning against these, saying we should cut off an appendage or pluck out an eye if necessary to prevent them. Jesus leaves no room for excusing sin, particularly sin against the vulnerable, or "little ones."

Action Step: Read Matthew 18:1–11, then answer the following question: Were you "one of these little ones" when wrong was done to you? Describe your situation.

Meditation: After advocating for the vulnerable ones of the human family, Jesus gives instructions on how to deal with offenses that occur between equals (notice the term is *brother*, indicating horizontality and equality). He counsels that we first approach the brother one-on-one. If this approach doesn't resolve the difference, we are to take one or two others. If this doesn't avail, we are to take it to the church. Confrontation is often part of the forgiveness process.

Notice that while Jesus commands one-on-one confrontation between equals, He doesn't require the weak and vulnerable to confront their wrongdoers. In relationships of equality, differences ideally are resolved between the two parties. In contrast, a power imbalance necessitates an advocate or a mediator.

In order to confront and forgive wrong, we must have a clear idea of what was done to us. Our feelings of outrage show that we have a sense of justice. True forgiveness builds from this foundation. To forgive intelligently and thoroughly, we must survey the damage.

Action Step: Make sure your grievances aren't imaginary. Some things we can overlook. Did the wrongdoer cause concrete physical, emotional, mental, social, spiritual, financial, and/or relational damage? Use those categories to delineate actual damage. If possible, let a trusted person who knows the situation review the worksheet and tell you if he or she concurs with your conclusions.

Survey the damage

Physical
Emotional
Mental
Social
Spiritual
Financial
Relational

Meditation: Some people, particularly victims of a family member, have a hard time admitting that others did wrong. Sometimes we want to justify those people. Or sometimes we ping-pong back and forth between excusing them and condemning them. A close relationship with the wrongdoer, and/or having had a high degree of trust, tends to compromise our perceptions. Yet we are told to "be sober," which includes admitting that people aren't angels (1 Peter 5:8). "All have sinned" (Romans 3:23), and "all flesh is as grass" (1 Peter 1:24). Don't be shocked that sinners sin. With the evidence of the above worksheet, admit that you were wronged.

Action Step: Now that you understand what forgiveness entails and you are fully aware of the damage, you can make an intelligent choice about whether to forgive or not. Below find a chart of the costs and the benefits of both forgiving the person and remaining in unforgiveness. This will help you to recognize the nature of forgiveness: it's a thoughtful decision as opposed to a whim or a feeling. List the effect that forgiving or not forgiving will have upon you, others, and God.

Forgiveness versus unforgiveness

Effect	Forgiveness costs	Forgiveness benefits	Unforgiveness costs	Unforgiveness benefits
On you				
On others				
On God				

Meditation: Matthew 18:21–35 relates a parable of forgiveness and debt collecting. A great land-owner calls one of his staff to account, saying he owes the equivalent of ten million dollars. The landowner orders him into prison, but the employee bows before him, saying, "Have patience, and I will pay you back!" (see verse 26). Then the landowner does something remarkable—he forgives the employee. Tragically, the employee fails to reflect the grace of his employer. He takes one of his own debtors by the throat, even though this person owes only about twenty dollars, and throws him into prison. This pushes the landowner beyond his limit. He angrily turns his employee over "to the torturers" (verse 34)! Jesus ends this parable by saying, "So My heavenly Father also will do to you if each of you, from his heart, does not forgive his brother his trespasses" (verse 35).

These are sobering, even frightening words. A little careful thinking reveals the psychology behind unforgiveness. Notice that the employee thought he could pay the landowner back, saying, "Have patience with me, and I will pay you all!" (verse 26). Denying the depth of his own sin, his hopeless debt, and his master's forgiveness, the employee has no basis from which to forgive his fellow man. Feeling righteous, he strangles and imprisons his brother.

Notice the debts in the parable. The debt between servant and master was ten million dollars; the debt between fellow men was about twenty dollars. While humans do indebt themselves to one another, these debts pale in comparison to the greatness of our debt to God.

Sociologic research shows that those who believe they could have done what their perpetrators did are more inclined to forgive. All are great debtors before God. Admit that you, too, are a sinner and have hurt God and others and are, carnally speaking, capable of great sin. "Humble yourselves, therefore, under God's mighty hand. . . . Cast all your anxiety on him because he cares for you" (1 Peter 5:6, 7, NIV). Choose to lay down your pride and self-righteousness.

Action Step: Using the worksheet below, recall the things you have done to others and God. This will help you to face your own sinful nature and increase your inclination to forgive others.

Things for which I have been forgiven

Whom did I hurt?	What did I do?	How did it affect them?

T
O
O
L
B
O
X

Whom did I hurt?	What did I do?	How did it affect them?

Action Step: Read Isaiah 53 out loud. Read with emotion, thinking carefully about each verse. Claim this promise: "If we confess our sins, He is faithful and just to forgive us our sins and to cleanse us from all unrighteousness" (1 John 1:9). Kneel down and confess your sin, then receive God's forgiveness and cleansing as a free gift, which you can't merit or earn.

Meditation: We sometimes cherish doubts of our own forgiveness. We may feel unforgiven even though we have confessed and forsaken our sin. Or we may have fallen into habitual sin in an attempt to cope with the pain of abuse. Faith comes to the rescue in all such cases. We must believe the promises of God and our own prayers. When we ask for bread, will our loving Father give us a stone (see Matthew 7:9)? He died to forgive us. Will He now withhold forgiveness when we ask? Likewise, if we ask for victory, will He not give it? To cherish doubt is to tarnish God's image. We must by faith embrace our forgiven and cleansed state. Expressing gratitude helps to accomplish this.

Action Step: Express gratitude. Sing such hymns as "Rejoice, Ye Pure in Heart" or "My Jesus, I Love Thee." Expression of your faith deepens impression. Read Psalm 103 aloud, thinking about how God has saved you from destruction.

Please note this: focusing on God's forgiveness of your sin does *not* minimize the other person's sin! It simply moves your focus from them to yourself, from a frustrating situation to a more productive situation. In psychology, we call this an *internal locus of control* versus an *external locus of control*.

Meditation: Now that your cup is full of forgiveness and gratitude, you are in a position to share it. You can choose to "send away" the wrong done to you and forgive the debt. This doesn't mean that you *forget* what was done. But you may think of it as boxing it and "sending it away" to a warehouse. Sin is like toxic waste. You are quarantining it by putting it away from yourself. In some cases, you will be able to tell the individual you have forgiven him or her. In other cases, especially where abuse is concerned, you will choose not to have any contact with the wrongdoer.

Forgiveness is a choice. You have set aside quality time to think carefully through this process. You have come to terms with what it means to forgive. You have surveyed the damage done to you; you have also acknowledged your own sin. You have received forgiveness. You have thanked God for that forgiveness. Now you are prepared to make the conscious, intelligent choice to forgive.

Action Step: Kneel down and pray, asking God to give you His Spirit as you choose to forgive. Pray for "those who spitefully use you" (Matthew 5:44). Mark the date on your calendar.

Meditation: You may have to revisit this decision. At times, you may feel overwhelmed with anger or other negative feelings. Remember that forgiveness is a choice to release the wrongdoer from a debt, send away this person's wrongdoing, and separate yourself from it. Expect to return to your decision and even walk through the steps again. It may take years before your feelings catch up to your choice. Don't get discouraged. Just because you feel hurt, angry, or offended doesn't mean that you chose those things. Remind yourself that you chose to forgive. Ever so slowly, those negative feelings will disappear.

FREEDOM-REMINDER EXERCISES

Doing things outside of our routine, preference, habit, and culture can be a great way to invigorate our sense of personal agency and the power of our choices. Do at least one freedom-reminder exercise per day!

- Get up at four o'clock in the morning and enjoy the world at its quietest.
- Make a card, write a kind paragraph, and send it to a friend.
- Take a hot bath and then go outside and roll in the snow or play in a sprinkler if there is no snow.
- Watch the sun rise or set.
- Play classical music loudly and pretend you are conducting.
- Play upbeat music very loud and dance as if no one is looking.
- Take a walk down a trail you have never walked before.
- Get a simple watercolor paint set and paint something beautiful.
- Make yourself a cup of tea.
- Take a nap when you normally wouldn't.
- Lie on your back and look at the sky for cloud pictures.
- Purchase a child's coloring book, and color a picture.
- Strike up a meaningful conversation in a random place.
- Find a prison ministry and attend.
- Try scuba diving or another sport.
- Get a pedicure.
- Get a massage.
- Go to an ethnic store and buy something.
- Take an alternate route to or from work.
- Wear something you wouldn't normally wear.
- Cut your hair really short or dye it a different color.
- Give a compliment.
- Go to a musical-instrument store and play the instruments.
- Join a seasonal choir.
- Take a short walk down your block and wave at your neighbors.
- Rather than ruminate on the wrongdoings of someone who has hurt you, list the good things he or she has done.
- Go to a different church, grocery store, or gas station—just for variety.
- Strike up a conversation with someone totally different from you just to understand his or her world a little bit.

- Love people the way they are instead of trying to change them.
- Listen to the political views of someone whose views differ from yours.
- Use only your left hand (or right, if you are left-handed) for an hour.

Worksheet 1

Lifetime goals: You are lying on your deathbed. Using the information from "My Personal Mission Statement" in the toolbox, what do you want to have accomplished in the following areas?

1. *Love.* What kinds of relationships do you want with your family, friends, and other relationships?
2. *Reputation.* How do you want the world to see you? How broad or small of an influence do you wish to have?
3. *Education.* What degree(s) or special training would you like to have obtained?
4. *Career.* What would you like to have accomplished in the realm of your work life?
5. *Creativity.* What special things would you like to have brought into existence?
6. *Money.* How much money would you like to have earned? How much money would you like to have spent? How much money would you like to have kept for posterity, if any? How much money would you like to have poured into missions?
7. *Special bucket-list items.* What special things would you like to have experienced or accomplished?

Ten-year goals: Ten years from now, you are looking back on your life. Answer the above questions for that time period.

Five-year goals: Five years from now, you are looking back on your life. Answer the above questions for that time period.

	Love	Reputation	Education	Career	Creativity	Money	Special Items
Lifetime							
Ten year							
Five year							

Worksheet 2

One-year goals: One year from now, you are looking back on your life. Answer the questions from worksheet 1, and create a list of specific, quantifiable goals for this time period.

One-month goals: One month from now, you are looking back on your life. Answer the questions from worksheet 1, and create a list of specific, quantifiable goals for this time period.

One-week goals: One week from now, you are looking back on your life. Answer the questions from worksheet 1, and create a list of specific, quantifiable goals for this time period.

Today's goals: One day from now, you are looking back on your life. Answer the questions from worksheet 1, and create a list of specific, quantifiable goals for this time period.

	Love	Reputation	Education	Career	Creativity	Money	Special Items
One year							
One month							

	Love	Reputation	Education	Career	Creativity	Money	Special Items
One week							
Today							

GOOD HABIT INVENTORY

Read the "Twelve Good Habits" worksheet in the toolbox. Next, rate your adherence to each habit on a scale of one to ten, with ten being the highest. Then plot your success over the next month.

	Week 1	Week 2	Week 3	Week 4
Rise early				
Spend time with God				
Eat breakfast				
Have a regular schedule				
Make a list of goals				
Eat healthy foods				
Drink lots of water				
Exercise				
Manage your thought life				
Manage your money				
Manage your time				
Connect with others				

How can you incorporate more gratitude into your daily life? Here are a few simple suggestions.

Write a thank-you note. Randomly and spontaneously, write someone a thank-you letter for the contributions this person has made to your life. Consider doing this regularly, such as once a month. For instance, try designating the first of the month as your gratitude letter day.

Keep a gratitude journal. Each day, write down at least three things for which you are grateful, and share them the next day with at least one person. Go ahead and tell this individual that it is a mental-health hack you use to keep your heart soft and happy.

Send someone a thank-you prayer. Even if you lack time to write, you can ask God to take your gratitude on the wings of prayer to someone who has blessed you. The next time you see this person, ask if he or she got it.

Count blessings with a friend. When friends talk, they often review the difficult and negative things in life. That's what friends are for, right? However, a shift toward discussing the positives in life might be a good thing and can keep the friendship from becoming a cesspool of negativity.

Pray about the positives. It's great that you can bring all your sorrows and complaints to the Almighty. But what about praising Him for the good? Enter into His courts with praise. Tell Him what has gone right, and ask for more.

Gratitude meditation. This exercise, which is explained on the next page, will help you focus on things for which you are grateful in a way that capitalizes on the benefits of meditation without putting your mind to sleep. It's mindfulness, not mindlessness, that we want!

GRATITUDE MEDITATION

Gratitude meditation uses the four beneficial aspects of meditation: breathing, focus, imagination, and objectivity. Rather than emptying the mind, it fills and focuses the mind on positive content. Gratitude meditation can be used whenever needed, but it is recommended that anxious people set aside ten minutes a day, preferably upon arising, for this exercise. Spend about two minutes on each segment.

Breathe

Sitting comfortably, begin breathing deeply and slowly while counting. Inhale (through your nose or mouth) for the count of six, hold for two counts, and exhale to the count of eight—each count being about a second. As you are able, slow your breathing down further and continue the exercise.

Focus

Focus your mind on something for which you are grateful. When other thoughts intrude, gently push them aside, telling yourself that for *now* you will focus on your gratitude. Move on to another and still another source of gratitude. Write down the three things you are grateful for, and remember to share them with someone later in the day.

Imagine

Direct your imagination toward future positive things, such as a visit to the beach, a family event, or the beauties and glories of heaven. Tell yourself that God is good and that the future will be blessed.

Think objectively

Consider the day ahead of you. If you feel a sense of anxiety, observe those feelings without coming to any conclusions about them. Tell yourself, "Feelings of fear do not define me; feelings of fear won't hurt me."

To amp up the spirituality of your meditation, choose a Bible verse. Savor the meaning of the verse, and think of how it applies to the here and now in your life. I recommended verses from Psalms, Proverbs, and the Gospel of John.

Mental distraction techniques

Here is a list of activities to provide a mental distraction:

- Count backward from one hundred by threes, sixes, or sevens, or count up by prime numbers or perfect squares.
- Sing "Row, Row, Row Your Boat" but leave a word off the end each time.
- Make an acronym out of your name with each letter describing one of your character qualities. Describe something you enjoy doing (cooking a favorite dish, planting a garden, etc.) in detail.
- Watch children's videos on YouTube, another website, or a DVD.
- Look at a current news article that is not likely to be upsetting or distressing.
- Distract yourself with *Tetris*, solitaire, sudoku, word searches, or other puzzle games.

Reorientation techniques

The following activities can help you reorient your thoughts:

- List reaffirming statements: "I am fine. God is good. I will make it through."
- Quote your favorite Bible verses out loud.
- Describe your surroundings in detail, including sights, sounds, smells, and temperature.
- Think about a fun time that you recently had with a friend. Call that friend, and talk about it with him or her.

Sensory-based techniques

The following ideas help you to concentrate on your senses:

- Run cool or warm water over your hands, or take a cool or warm bath or shower.
- Spray yourself with your favorite perfume, and focus on the scent.
- Feel the weight of your body in your chair or on the floor.
- Play with a fidget toy, key ring, or a tiny plushy.
- Bite into a lemon, orange, or lime, or suck on a sour or minty candy or an ice cube.
- Drink a warm or cool drink.
- Place a cool washcloth on your face, or hold something cold, such as a can of soda.
- Dance to soothing music.
- Hug another person.

GROUNDING TECHNIQUES (cont.)

Movement-based techniques

These techniques can help you to feel more grounded through movement:

- Breathe deeply and slowly, and count your breaths.
- Grab tightly onto a chair, or press your feet against the ground as firmly as you can.
- Rub your palms and clap your hands, or wiggle your toes.
- Stretch out your arms or legs, roll your head on your neck, or clench and unclench your fists.
- Stomp your feet, walk around, run, jump, ride a bike, or do jumping jacks.
- Squeeze a pillow, stuffed animal, or ball.
- Play with a pet.
- Color in a coloring book, finger-paint, or draw anything that comes to mind.
- Pop some bubble wrap, or blow and pop actual bubbles.
- Dig in the dirt or a garden, jump on a pile of leaves, or splash around in puddles.[1]

---

1. This tool is adapted from "Grounding Techniques," DID Research, last updated December 16, 2017, http://did-research .org/treatment/grounding.html.

Try to imagine yourself in each situation, then rate the likelihood that you would react in the way described.[1]

1. Very unlikely
2. Unlikely
3. Slightly unlikely
4. About 50 percent likely
5. Slightly likely
6. Likely
7. Very likely

_____ 1. Your boss confidentially tells you that your work performance is poor. What is the likelihood that you will try to improve your work performance?

_____ 2. After realizing you have received too much change at a store, you decide to keep it because the salesclerk didn't notice. What is the likelihood that you would feel uncomfortable about keeping the money?

_____ 3. Your boss criticizes you in front of your coworkers because your rudeness to a patron led to that person filing a complaint about you. What is the likelihood that you would make up a reason to leave work?

_____ 4. You rip a recipe out of a magazine while waiting in a doctor's office. The receptionist notices and makes a disapproving face. What is the likelihood that this would make you would feel like a bad person?

_____ 5. You secretly cheat on your taxes. What is the likelihood that you would feel remorse about breaking the law?

_____ 6. You arrive late to a presentation and lose the contract with the company due to your lateness. What is the likelihood that you would feel like a hopelessly disorganized person?

_____ 7. A friend censures you for being rude. What is the likelihood that you would stop spending time with that friend?

_____ 8. Friends knock on your door for a surprise visit on Sunday morning, but you are still dozing in bed and the house is a mess. What is the likelihood you pretend not to be home?

_____ 9. You reveal a friend's secret, though your friend never finds out. What is the likelihood that your failure to keep the secret would lead you to exert extra effort to keep secrets in the future?

_____ 10. You falsify a damage report to get more money from a home-insurance claim. What is the likelihood that you would think you are a despicable human being?

_____ 11. You strongly defend a point of view in a continuing-education class, and later, through reflection, realize you were wrong. What is the likelihood that this would make you think more carefully before you speak?

_____ 12. You mistakenly accuse a retail outlet of falsely charging your credit card but later you remember that you really had purchased something. What is the likelihood that you would feel like a terrible person?

_____ 13. You take home some supplies from the office and are caught by your boss. What is the likelihood that this would lead you to quit your job?

_____ 14. At a party, you drop a hot appetizer on a table, and it leaves a mark. You neglect to mention it to the host. What is the likelihood that you would later realize that you should have said something?

_____ 15. While in conflict with family members, you suddenly realize you are being very grumpy and critical. What is the likelihood that you would try to act more considerately toward your loved ones?

_____ 16. You lie to people but they never find out about it. What is the likelihood that you would feel terrible about the lies you told?

Talley up your answers and follow these instructions.

For your level of guilt awareness, add up your answers to questions 2, 5, 14, 16.

For your level of willingness to repair guilt, add up your answers to questions 1, 9, 11, 15.

For your level of shame awareness, add up your answers to questions 4, 6, 10, 12.

For your tendency to withdraw from shame, add up your answers to questions 3, 7, 8, 13.

The higher the number the more guilt, shame, and so on, you are aware of or feel.

While both shame and guilt indicate moral sensitivity, one's proneness to feeling shame is associated with more distressing emotions than the proneness toward feeling guilt. This is because we tend to repair guilt but withdraw from shame.

---

1. This tool is adapted from Taya R. Cohen, "Guilt and Shame Proneness Scale," Carnegie Mellon University, August 1, 2011, https://www.cmu.edu/tepper/faculty-and-research/assets/docs/guilt-shame-proneness-gasp-scale-aug-2011.pdf.

This worksheet is based on the classic book *Steps to Christ* by Ellen G. White. For a more comprehensive understanding, get yourself a copy and read it!

Let's talk about getting to know God. I recommend taking a day for each step. Use the questions and directions below as a guide.

Behold. Take some time to watch God from a distance.

- What does God say about His character? Exodus 33:18, 19
- Recount a time when you saw God in nature.
- Recount a time when you saw God reveal Himself in a close, bonded human relationship.
- What favorite story from the life of Jesus conveys His love?
- In your own words, blending together the last three answers, what is God like?
- What was God's ultimate expression of self-sacrificing love? Isaiah 53:5; Matthew 27:46
- Was the purpose of the Cross to create in God's heart a love for humanity? 2 Corinthians 5:19
- Could anyone or anything else have accomplished our redemption? John 3:16

Be aware. Contemplate the condition of sinful humanity and our great need for God.

- Have you ever felt guilt, shame, or both? Recount that time.
- What did you do to cope with those feelings?
- Once in a sinful condition, humanity couldn't enjoy God's holy presence. Why? Romans 8:7
- How does God bring us back into a condition that allows us to enjoy His presence? John 3:3
- Is it possible for us to change our own hearts? Job 14:4
- Humanism says that in order to be good, we need only develop what's inside of us. Is this true? 1 Corinthians 2:4, 5
- What action can we take to give God access into our hearts? Matthew 6:33
- Is there any true excellence of character apart from Christ? James 1:17
- Is there access to God through any other than Christ? John 14:6

Be broken. Understand and appreciate God's gift of transformative repentance.

- What was the first thing Peter said when, at Pentecost, many cried, "What shall we do?" Acts 2:38
- True repentance is more than regretting the consequences of sin. What biblical characters only cared about that?

HOW TO KNOW GOD (cont.)

- What biblical character had an exemplary repentance experience? Psalm 32:1, 2
- David asked God to create what within him? Psalm 51:10
- Does the Bible say we should repent first, then come to God, or come as we are? Matthew 11:28
- How does the Bible describe repentance—as something we conjure up or receive as a gift? Acts 5:31
- What draws us to God more than anything else? John 12:32
- "If he [the sinner] does not resist, he will be drawn to Jesus."[1] Are there ways you are resisting? What are they?
- Pride feels no need for God. But when we realize our sinfulness, how will we pray? Luke 18:13
- Can we become good enough to come to Jesus? Jeremiah 13:23

Be honest. Learn the beauty of being real with God and other people.

- What are two main ways we can handle our sin? Proverbs 28:13
- Does the Bible say we should even be real with each other about our sins? James 5:16
- When we find ourselves broken over our sin, how does God respond? Psalm 34:18
- We confess some sins to God and some to others. Write a list of the things you should make right with other people.
- Should we confess and then expect to repeat history, or can we change? Isaiah 1:16, 17
- Is it our natural inclination to admit fault or to evade it by blaming others? Genesis 3:12, 13
- How will God transform our attitudes about our personal histories? 1 Timothy 1:15
- What has God promised about confession? 1 John 1:9

Be blessed. Develop the art of a healthy devotional life.

- How much of the heart must be yielded to God in order to be transformed? Jeremiah 29:13
- How did the prophet Isaiah describe our natural condition? Isaiah 1:5, 6
- Is our surrender based on a blind submission, or does God work with our reason? Isaiah 1:18
- Idols get in the way of surrender, including the idols of materialism, status, and ease. What are your idols?
- Ask yourself this question: What has Christ given for me? Write down your answers.
- All we really give up for Jesus are sin-polluted hearts. How do we feel when we hesitate to make that surrender?

- In order to surrender yourself to God, you need to understand the true force of the will. Do you?
- You can choose to serve God. You can give Him your will. Will you, right now?

Believe. Take a step in faith.

- God offers us His peace and freedom from sin at what cost to us? Isaiah 55:1
- What does God do to our sin? Isaiah 1:18
- What does God give us in exchange for our naturally stony, selfish hearts? Ezekiel 36:26
- After you repent, confess, and surrender your will, you believe God has forgiven you because He _____.
- We learn how Jesus forgives sin by witnessing how He healed disease. What truths emerge from the story in John 5:5–9?
- What happens when we act in response to God's promise? Mark 11:24
- Once we have been forgiven and cleansed by Jesus, do we need to tremble in shame before God? Romans 8:1
- Now that you have received Jesus, what should you do day by day? Colossians 2:6
- Thousands fail because they don't believe Jesus pardons them personally. Do you?
- The parable of the prodigal son teaches us about God. What did the father do when he saw his son coming? Luke 15:18–20

Be accountable. Obey the One who loves you.

- Does conversion always occur at a specific point in time? John 3:8
- Can we originate love for God in our own hearts? 1 John 4:7–9
- Two great spiritual errors are *salvation by works* and *salvation in sin*. Which one tempts you?
- What kind of obedience does God call us to? Hebrews 10:16
- If we abide in Jesus, what will be our attitude toward sin? 1 John 3:5, 6
- How do we know whether we know God? 1 John 2:3, 6
- According to Galatians 2:20, the faith of Jesus led Him to _____ us and _____ _____ for us.
- The faith of Jesus contrasts with the faith of demons. What kind of faith do demons have? James 2:19
- How will a person who has been born again feel about the law of God? Psalm 119:97
- Jesus would like us not to sin, but if we do, what does He do for us? 1 John 2:1

Become. Enjoy the process of growth in Christ.

- Isaiah 61:3 calls us "trees of righteousness." What are some parallels between tree growth and spiritual growth?
- Mark 4:28 says we grow like a cornstalk. How are those two processes similar?
- Meditate on this: we grow when we receive the sun and rain from God. Isaiah 60:1, 2, 9; Psalm 84:11; Hosea 14:5
- How do we abide in Christ? Colossians 2:6
- Try praying each morning upon arising, laying your life before God in surrender.
- What has Jesus promised for the weary? Matthew 11:28, 29
- The enemy tempts us with the pleasures of the world, the cares of life, the faults of others, and our own failings. Which do you succumb to?
- The enemy tempts conscientious people to dwell on their own mistakes. Are you one of them?
- Has God promised to grow us? 2 Corinthians 3:18
- According to Philippians 2:13, if Christ is dwelling in our hearts, what will He will do in us?

Be a servant. Serve others, and be blessed.

- What example did Jesus leave us regarding serving others? Matthew 20:28
- Can you recall a time when you tried to bless someone else and ended up being blessed yourself?
- According to 2 Corinthians 8:9, the more we sacrifice, the more we become like Jesus. He was rich but became poor for our sakes. Why?
- Trying to maintain the Christian life by passively accepting blessings but doing nothing is like eating without _____.
- Do we need to go to foreign lands to do God's work? 1 Corinthians 7:24
- Should we excuse ourselves from making a contribution if we are not extremely gifted?
- Do we need to worry about what other people think of our service for Jesus? Colossians 1:21–23

Be a student. Read God's story.

- Nature is one of God's "books." When have you seen God's character displayed in His creation?

- Is nature a full revelation of how beautiful heaven will be? 1 Corinthians 2:9
- Another of God's "books" is His providence and care in our lives. Name a time when you noticed God's care for you.
- The clearest revelation of God is in His Word. What is your favorite book of the Bible?
- Who is the central figure of the Bible, and what is its central message? John 1:3; 5:39; Revelation 22:12
- What is in God's Word? John 6:63
- Is the Bible only for scholarly people or common people?
- Meditating on one passage of Scripture benefits us more than skimming large portions. What is your favorite passage?

Beseech. Talk to your heavenly Father.

- God speaks to us, but to be truly connected, we must speak to Him too. Do you talk to God as to a friend?
- Do you believe Jesus needed to pray? If so, why?
- God pours out His blessing like rain on people in what condition? Isaiah 44:3
- While our need is our great argument, what must we do to open the door for our need to be met? Matthew 7:7
- How do you know that God will give you the blessings you need? Romans 8:32
- What accompanies effective prayer? Mark 11:24
- What attitude toward those who have hurt us should accompany effective prayer? Matthew 6:12
- Why, do you think, does God tell us to persevere in prayer?
- What is God's spirit and attitude toward our neediness? Psalm 147:3
- Should we express only our needs in prayer, or is there something else we should express? Deuteronomy 12:7

Be wise. When doubts come knocking, we are to seek wisdom from God.

- God doesn't ask us to believe without evidence, yet He leaves room for doubt. Why, do you think, does He do this?
- What does God's Word say about our ability to understand everything about Him? Job 11:7, 8; Romans 11:33
- What sometimes happens when inexperienced people come upon a difficult Bible text? 2 Peter 3:16

- What kind of heart condition should we guard against? Hebrews 3:12
- What do you believe is ultimately responsible for the doubts that destroy a person's faith?
- Who alone can know all there is to know about God? Colossians 2:2, 3; 1 Corinthians 2: 10, 11
- What has God promised regarding the truth we need to understand? John 16:13, 14
- What choice puts us in a condition to understand the Word of God? John 7:17
- How does God feel about us testing His promises in order to decide whether to believe? Psalm 34:8

Be joyful. Eternal happiness has the last word.

- Jesus sends us out into the world to share His love. Whom does He speak to through us? 2 Corinthians 3:2, 3
- What shows us that God would sacrifice anything for our eternal happiness? Romans 8:32
- Is it possible to live focused ourselves, caring only for ourselves, and truly thrive? Romans 14:7
- What is the word most often used to indicate that we should depend fully upon God? Psalm 37:3
- Did Jesus promise us that only good things would happen? John 16:33; 17:15
- What object lessons did Jesus use to describe God's care for us? Matthew 6:26
- Do we have a choice whether to fear or not? John 14:27
- Did Jesus want us to have a little bit of joy, a medium amount of joy, or a lot of joy? John 15:11
- What will Jesus finally say to us when it is time to enter the land of eternal joy? Matthew 25:34

---

1. Ellen G. White, *Steps to Christ* (Oakland, CA: Pacific Press®, 1892), 27.

Making friends

The first step in making friends is *choosing a forum*. Befriending someone is easier in the right context. So what are some healthy friend-making forums? Here are some suggestions:

- Book clubs
- Hobby clubs
- Service organizations
- Meetup.com
- Neighbors
- Dog parks
- Cultural events
- Sports classes
- Seminars
- Self-improvement groups
- Public-speaking clubs
- Religious organizations

The second step in making friends is to *come from a place of abundance*. You may be lonely, but don't put all of your social needs on one person or you will scare him or her away. Even if you are alone in the world, God loves you. You are standing in a reservoir of heavenly relational generosity. Take that love, which God says He will pour into you, and share it. Think of friendship as creating tributaries of this great reservoir. In this way, you will not only receive from friendships but also give something.

Third, *learn the art of conversation*. Don't be afraid of this step. A few simple principles and the courage to learn by trial and error are all you need.

The essential principle is serving others. Take an interest in people—not in a nosey way but in a way that makes them feel like they matter. Don't go too deep too fast, though. Think of conversation as an onion with layers. Let the layers come off gradually and slowly. Think of it also as a tennis game where the ball bounces back and forth. You say something, the other person says something, then back to you, and so on. Avoid monologuing or just sitting quietly while the other person monopolizes the conversation unless you can't stop him or her, which happens.

Finally, *find the friends who are hiding in plain sight*. Sometimes the best potential friends are the people we are around all the time. Strike up conversations at work or other places where you have learned to ignore people. You can also try reviving an old friendship, calling people you have lost touch with to see how they are doing. And what about the old-fashioned practice of befriending your neighbors? Bring them a small gift, introduce yourself, and let them know you are there for them in a neighborly way.

Keeping friends

The first step in keeping friends is *allowing for challenges*. Relationships can't really deepen without some conflict, so just accept it as an inevitable part of living authentically. Some of us have had such a negative experience with conflict in relationships that we flee as soon as a ripple of disagreement comes. There's no need for that! Press through by learning to resolve conflict.

Second, *resolve conflict*. One of the most important de-escalators in conflict is good listening. Remember that you don't have to agree with the person, but you do need to understand him or her. Use the EAR technique to learn active listening. Often that's all people really want—to be understood. For a more structured approach, there's a wonderful communication tool—the floor technique—that can radically catalyze conflict resolution.

The third step in keeping friends is to *keep investing*. Sometimes we take one another for granted. We tend to work the hardest for relationships we may or may not keep and neglect the ones we know will always be there. James Taylor said, "Shower the people you love with love. Show them the way that you feel. Things are gonna work out fine if you only will."[1]

Finally, *forgive*. Sooner or later, every loved one will do something to harm us. And we will probably do something to harm them. Forgiveness is basic to relationships. Really all we are doing in forgiving others is sharing from the wealth of forgiveness that God has given us. The same door that receives forgiveness lets it flow out to others. Open the door, and keep the grace flowing.

And remember, forgiveness is more than an event. It's a way of life. Maya Angelou said, "It's one of the greatest gifts you can give yourself, to forgive. Forgive everybody."[2] Norman Cousins said, "Life is an adventure in forgiveness."[3] Martin Luther King Jr. said, "Forgiveness is not an occasional act, it's a permanent attitude."[4] Make forgiveness a part of who you are.

---

1. James Taylor, "Shower the People," track 1 of *In the Pocket*, Warner Bros. Records, 1976.
2. Maya Angelou, "Oprah Talks to Maya Angelou," interview by Oprah Winfrey, *O, the Oprah Magazine*, May 2013, https://www.oprah.com/omagazine/maya-angelou-interviewed-by-oprah-in-2013/5.
3. Norman Cousins, "Editor's Odyssey: Gleanings From Articles and Editorials by N.C.," *Saturday Review*, April 15, 1975, 12.
4. Martin Luther King Jr., quoted in Johann Christoph Arnold, *Why Forgive?* (Walden, NY: Plough Publishing, 2010), 188, 189.

In order to discover your personal mission statement, first, underline *all* the entries that apply to you in each of the categories.

Values	Passions	Gifts
Accomplishment	Advocating for animal rights	Arts
Adventure	Assisting people in improving their health	Communication
Beauty	Creating beautiful art, music, and/or literature	Computer technology
Challenge	Delivering life-saving messages	Crafts
Cleanliness, orderliness	Fighting crime	Critical thinking
Collaboration	Helping build functional, healthy churches	Decision making
Communication	Helping find cures for disease	Discernment
Community	Helping people find emotional healing	Drawing
Concern for others	Helping people in their relationships	Financial management
Creativity	Helping the needy	Humor
Discipline	Increasing Bible literacy	Innovation
Diversity	Ministering to a marginalized group	Instrumental music
Efficiency	Promoting education	Languages
Equality	Promoting family values	Marketing and promotions
Excellence	Reaching out to lonely people	Math
Fairness	Righting social injustices	Music composition
Faith	Scientific research	Networking
Family	Teaching, dispensing important information	Peacemaker
Freedom	Teaching parenting	Photography
Fun	Working for the cause of civil rights	Physical coordination
Gratitude	Working for the cause of religious liberty	Physical strength
Hard work	Other _____	Poetry
Honesty, integrity		Problem solving
Individuality		Project management
Innovation		Public speaking
Knowledge		Singing
Loyalty		Social skills
Personal growth		Storytelling
Practicality		Writing
Privacy		Other _____
Prosperity		
Reliability		
Respect		
Service to others		
Simplicity		

Values	Passions	Gifts
Social justice Status Strength Tradition Trust Truth Other _____		

Next, choose three underlined selections from each category, and write them down.

Values	Passions	Gifts
1.	1.	1.
2.	2.	2.
3.	3.	3.

Now plug those selections into the following sentence:

From motivations of _____, _____,
and _____, and a passion for _____,
_____, and _____, I will use my gifts of
_____, _____, and _____ to
change the world.

Rework this statement until it feels right, and then start sharing it.

Answer each question with a number indicating how strongly you agree, with zero being the lowest and three the highest.[1] Tally your points at the end of the assessment to determine how strong you are on the posttraumatic growth scale.

If you have a low rating, don't be upset. Through the grace of Jesus, you can redirect into a healthier mind-set.

Appreciation of life	0	1	2	3
I have a clear sense of my life's priorities.				
I value my own life more than ever.				
I appreciate each day more than ever.				

Relationships with others	0	1	2	3
I know I can count on people.				
I feel closer to other people.				
I am more willing to express my feelings to other people.				
I have more compassion for other people.				
I put more effort into relationships.				
I value other people more.				
I am better at accepting that I need people.				

New possibilities in life	0	1	2	3
I have developed new interests.				
I have established a new path going forward.				
I actually have new opportunities since the trauma.				
I am more likely to try to change things that need changing.				

TOOLBOX

Personal strength	0	1	2	3
I have confidence that I will make the right choice.				
I know I can handle difficulties.				
I will be able to do better things with my life than before.				
The trauma has opened up new opportunities.				
I am even more likely to try to change things since the trauma.				

Spiritual change	0	1	2	3
I understand spiritual things better than I did.				
I have a stronger religious faith than I did.				

Scoring

0–20: Consider professional counseling.

21–36: Work on redirecting your beliefs to more hopeful channels.

37–63: Keep looking up, and share your special ability for growth with other people.

---

1. This tool is adapted from Richard G. Tedeschi and Lawrence G. Calhoun, "The Posttraumatic Growth Inventory: Measuring the Positive Legacy of Trauma," *Journal of Stress* 9, no. 3 (1996): 455–471.

This simple exercise should noticeably relax yet invigorate you. If this is done faithfully, it should work as well as a pill to ward off a panic attack or other experience of anxiety.

Sitting comfortably, begin breathing deeply and slowly while counting. To create resistance, purse your lips as if you were breathing through a very thin straw. Some people like to inhale and exhale through pursed lips; others like to inhale through the nose and exhale through the mouth. Inhale to the count of six, hold for two counts, and exhale to the count of eight, with each count being about a second. As you are able, slow down your breathing further. Take the opportunity during this quiet time to praise God and thank Him for the blessings He has given to you.

Next, gradually tense and release all the muscles in your body:

1. Tense your muscles while inhaling.
2. Release your muscles while exhaling.
3. Release the muscles in the following sequence: Right foot, right lower leg and foot, entire right leg; left foot, left lower leg and foot, entire left leg; right hand, right forearm and hand, entire right arm; left hand, left forearm and hand, entire left arm; abdomen, chest, neck, and shoulders.

The Sabbath celebrates the birthday of the world. Genesis 2:1–3 says, "Thus the heavens and the earth, and all the host of them, were finished. And on the seventh day God ended His work which He had done, and He rested on the seventh day from all His work which He had done. Then God blessed the seventh day and sanctified it."

The Sabbath also celebrates our redemption. Deuteronomy 5:15 says, "And remember that you were a slave in the land of Egypt, and the Lord your God brought you out from there by a mighty hand and by an outstretched arm; therefore the Lord your God commanded you to keep the Sabbath day." Because of these realities, the Sabbath can be the happiest day of the week.

Here are some practical suggestions to make it everything it can be:

- Spend time in corporate worship, coming before God in awe and wonder.
- Spend time in fellowship, nurturing your relationships with family, friends, and the faith community.
- Spend time in meditation and study, enjoying the themes of God's Word.
- Spend time in nature, surrounding yourself with God's creation.
- Spend time making music, whether in a church context or more casually.
- Spend time enjoying special foods that you wouldn't have every day, a bouquet of flowers, or special toys for kids.

Develop creative ways of making the Sabbath special:

- Light scented candles to make your house smell fabulous.
- Set up an "Alleluia Café" for Friday night supper: the children design and serve the menu, the parents order the food, and everything is free.
- After supper, have each person at the table share a blessing from the week.
- Have a special Sabbath backpack for each child, with special books, a small Bible, binoculars, bottles of water, and coloring books and crayons.
- Encourage each child to use the crayons and paper to illustrate the worship talk or sermon.
- Go on a prayer walk around your neighborhood, praying for each neighbor.
- Play Bible charades: Split into teams and have each team silently act out a Bible story while the other team guesses.
- Take a trip to a special beach or forest and walk.
- Have an in-home or church concert in which every person sings a song or recites a poem.
- Take time to reach out to people with whom you have lost touch.
- Work on a gratitude scrapbook with pictures of fond memories.

- Get out the play dough and other crafts.
- Engage in a service project, such as feeding the homeless.

The following resources have more great ideas:

- May-Ellen Colón, *From Sundown to Sundown: How to Keep the Sabbath and Enjoy It!* (Nampa, ID: Pacific Press®, 2008).
- Karen Holford, *100 Creative Activities for Sabbath* (Nampa, ID: Pacific Press®, 2005).
- Glen Robinson, *52 Things to Do on Sabbath* (Hagerstown, MD: Review and Herald®, 1999).
- Don Pate, *52 Sabbath Activities for Teen Groups* (Hagerstown, MD: Review and Herald®, 1995).

Solomon said, "Catch us the foxes, the little foxes that spoil the vines, for our vines have tender grapes" (Song of Solomon 2:15). It's often the little things—the habits, reactions, and character traits—that make or break a life or relationship. The list below will give you a chance to ask the Holy Spirit to catch your personal "foxes" for you.[1] Pray Psalm 139:23, 24:

> Search me, O God, and know my heart;
> Try me, and know my anxieties;
> And see if there is any wicked way in me,
> And lead me in the way everlasting.

Criticism

Humans tend to focus on problems. This trait often takes the form of picking on (or severely gouging) other people. Criticism raises us up as we drag others down, but the lift doesn't last. We become junkies who need stronger and stronger criticism fixes to support insatiable, misaligned egos.

Replace criticism with affirmation. I tell critical people to go on a criticism fast in which they can't criticize anyone or anything (including themselves) for three weeks. After this, when they wish to criticize, they must create an *affirmation sandwich* in which they affirm before criticizing and follow the critique with another affirmation. Soon they develop a taste for affirmation and decide to do it more often.

Complaining

Closely related to criticism, complaining entails a lifestyle of pointing out and dwelling upon the negative, unfortunate, and difficult to the exclusion of the positive and pleasant. At the foundation of this grumbling lifestyle lies a sense of entitlement in which we believe that the world, God, or society owe us a good time.

Replace complaining with gratitude. Gratitude flows from a heart that understands its unworthiness; all good things become gifts rather than entitlements. It is helpful to think of three things for which one is grateful before going to sleep at night and three more upon arising in the morning. This habit will almost always result in a complete cure.

Self-pity

Playing the victim or feeling sorry for oneself actually deepens pain and prevents healing of emotional scars. The horrible reality of victimization can be prolonged when we dwell on it unnecessarily. In so doing, we remain victims by reinforcing our feelings of powerlessness.

Replace self-pity with taking responsibility. I like to say, "It's not your fault, but it is your responsibility." This means that you have a choice in your reaction to suffering and misfortune. Often dramatic growth and freedom come when people finally transition from a victim mentality into a mind-set of taking responsibility. Begin by listing five things you can do to improve your situation, then ask a friend or other accountability partner to help you act upon those things.

Worry

In psychology, worry is called *hypervigilance.* The dangerous world in which we live presents many threats to our well-being. Our fear mechanism comes in handy when faced with these threats; adrenaline helps us to fight or fly out of danger, which is all well and good. But when we react to the possibility of danger, rather than actual danger, we carry the fear into our everyday experience, and the fear itself becomes a threat. More than this, it does absolutely nothing to protect us; in fact, it often serves as a self-fulfilling prophecy that brings about the very event that we dreaded! Ellen White said, "Worry is blind, and cannot discern the future."[2] We worry because we think we are protecting ourselves, but we aren't.

Replace worry with trust. "God is faithful; he will not let you be tempted beyond what you can bear. But when you are tempted, he will also provide a way out so that you can endure it." (1 Corinthians 10:13, NIV). As we walk forward in faith and trust, we refute our own worst imaginings. You may want to begin by confining your worrying to one hour a day and gradually reduce the amount of time to zero.

Avoidance

Many people know what they should do but avoid doing it, as if subjecting themselves to anything unpleasant or even just boring would cause an immediate, irreversible psychological meltdown. Often people say they are not motivated to do a certain activity—exercise, talk to a specific person, read the Bible, and so on—but they are motivated to avoid doing those things.

Replace avoidance with action. Exercise your God-given will. The amazing thing about the will is that it moves independent of inclination. In other words, we can choose to do the opposite of what we feel inclined to do. *Opposite action* is used in dialectical behavioral therapy to redirect a weak or perverted will that is found in such conditions as borderline personality disorder. It involves choosing to move in the opposite direction of inclination. To retrain your will, do three beneficial things per day that you are disinclined to do. Start small; baby steps count!

Emotionalism

Many people, especially those of a sensitive, passionate nature, live by their emotions. One aspect of this is emotional reasoning, which is the belief that if one feels something is true, it must be true. Many thus feel their way into dangerous relationships and situations and later reap the bitter harvest. Then they believe the ensuing feelings of doom and despair and lose hope. Our feelings are like children—precious but not capable of driving our car.

Replace emotionalism with reason. Reason doesn't make a person into Mr. Spock or the Tin Man, by the way. Reason actually makes a person more capable of deep emotion. Basing one's choices on timeless life principles provides an anchor that enables a person to stay safe in the deepest waters of the churning sea of life. When an individual has such an anchor, he or she needn't hug the shore out of fear of shipwreck. I use cognitive behavioral therapy to help people learn to use their reasoning powers with excellent results.

Bitterness

Often very painful chapters of life threaten to consume us. Moving on can be difficult and slow even for the most forgiving. Some people gain satisfaction in rehearsing the hurtful events repeatedly, even attempting to gain sympathizers and turn others against their enemy. Truly hurtful people should be exposed to help spare others, and the pain of abuse must be processed. But take care not to overprocess the pain.

Replace bitterness with forgiveness. Hebrews 12:15 ties receiving the grace of God to not allowing bitterness to take root in our hearts. *Grace* is unmerited favor and undeserved forgiveness and is freely bestowed. Jesus forgave His enemies, and so can we. We don't need to trust them, excuse them, or turn a blind eye to the wrong done. Forgiveness is an intelligent choice to release someone from punishment because we ourselves have been released, and it is a freeing, joyful alternative to the tangled root of bitterness.

The seven deadly psychological sins

Here is a summary of the seven deadly psychological sins and their replacements. Fill out the inventory below to direct your process of change:

Sin	Replacement
Criticism	Affirmation
Complaining	Gratitude
Self-pity	Taking responsibility
Worry	Trust
Avoidance	Action
Emotionalism	Reason
Bitterness	Forgiveness

"Therefore confess your sins to each other and pray for each other so that you may be healed. The prayer of a righteous person is powerful and effective" (James 5:16, NIV).

Confess

Rate yourself from one to ten (ten being the most) on the following deadly psychological sins.

Sin	1–10
Criticism	
Complaining	
Self-pity	
Worry	
Avoidance	
Emotionalism	
Bitterness	

Prayer

Pray the following prayer, filling in the blanks.

Dear God,

   I realize I have a problem with _____. Here is how it usually occurs: _____

_____

_____

_____

_____

_____.

   God, give me Your grace to change. I claim the promise, "The love of God has been poured out in our hearts by the Holy Spirit who was given to us" (Romans 5:5). Filled with Your love, I pray I will replace _____ with _____ and day by day be more completely conformed to Your image.

---

1. This tool is based on Jennifer Jill Schwirzer, "7 Psychological Pitfalls and How to Fix Them," Life and Health Network, July 11, 2017, https://lifeandhealth.org/lifestyle/7-psychological-pitfalls-and-how-to-fix-them/118011.html.
2. Ellen G. White, *The Desire of Ages* (Nampa, ID: Pacific Press®, 2002), 330.

We are made in the image of a relational God, designed to love and be loved.[1] Yet we also seem mysteriously wired toward dysfunction in our relationships. How can we get back to what we are meant to be? Beyond the obvious relationship sins, such as stealing, infidelity, murder, abuse, and lying, what are the subtler practices that break our bonds? Finding and replacing them is worth the effort and will be rewarded with much more happiness, peace, and love, love, love!

Escalation

A study from 2002 suggests that hostility levels may be better predictors of one's heart disease risk than traditional factors, such as high cholesterol, high blood pressure, smoking, and being over-weight.[2] Another study showed that the type of anger matters when it comes to health: constructive anger protects against coronary heart disease, but destructive anger was destructive.[3] A Bible writer chimes in on this one too: "Be angry, and do not sin" (Psalm 4:4).

Often escalation takes place within the context of well-established reactive cycles in a relation-ship. In my observation, the only way out is up. If either person in an escalated situation will take a moment to pray, even within his or her own heart, this individual will effectively break the cycle by redirecting his or her focus and energy vertically instead of horizontally. This person will also be un-der the influence of God, who can help us respond with wisdom and prudence rather than temper.

Invalidation

The next deadly relationship sin is invalidation. Unlike escalation, invalidation can be quite sub-tle. Often it comes in the form of trying to help: "Don't worry," "Don't be angry," or "Don't cry." Research conducted by Scott Stanley, Daniel Trathen, Milt Bryan, and Savanna McCain revealed four negative patterns that were (1) present in almost all failed relationships, (2) strong predictors of divorce, (3) often learned from the home of origin, and (4) tend to neutralize all the good that might be going on in the relationship. Here are the four patterns:

1. Escalation
2. Invalidation
3. Negative interpretation
4. Withdrawal[4]

The best replacement for invalidation is empathic listening. James 1:19 says, "Let every man be swift to hear, slow to speak, slow to wrath." Most of us are slow to hear, quick to speak, and quick to wrath—in other words, escalation. The Behavioral Change Stairway model, developed by the Federal Bureau of Investigation's Crisis Negotiation Unit, which specializes in hostage situations, is a dialoguing method that involves five stages:

1. Active listening
2. Empathy
3. Rapport
4. Influence
5. Behavioral change

If active listening can begin the process of calming a hostage situation, it can help our lesser conflicts! Most people don't want others simply to agree with them. They want to be understood and *felt*. Rather than invalidating, try active listening and empathy, and a whole new world of communication will open up.

Defensiveness
Arguably, the reigning king of marriage therapy is John Gottman, who is the creator of what he calls the "Four Horsemen of the Apocalypse." These "horsemen" are four traits Gottman noticed in marriages headed for separation and divorce. The four horsemen are

1. criticism,
2. contempt,
3. defensiveness, and
4. stonewalling.[5]

Some defensiveness can be healthy. It's a pattern of defensiveness we want to avoid. If people you love feel that they cannot raise issues, express feelings, request changes, or talk about future plans, then you have likely developed a pattern of defensiveness. What's missing? True, active, open communication.

The replacement behavior for defensiveness? Openness. Receptivity. The very perceived attacks you think are so devastating might actually carry helpful information. Now, I am not talking about accepting or being open to verbal abuse or anything of the sort. I am talking about being open to the needs and requests of caring, loving people in our lives.

Often distorted beliefs get in the way of being open to change. Perhaps we think, *I should always be perfect*; *people should always be totally satisfied with their relationships*; or *if someone isn't happy with me, I have failed*. These distorted, extreme beliefs—many of them formed when we were young—form the cognitive foundation for a habit of defensiveness.

Openness goes directly against the grain of our tendency to protect our own agendas. Once people get used to being open, they start to like it, and often those who may have been critical will be more generous as well.

Voilà! Defensiveness gone. Communication happening. Love flowing.

Withdrawal

Human beings are social creatures, created in the image of a God of relationships. Because of this, we are programmed innately with certain social needs. We can't deprive ourselves of these needs and be healthy any more than we can deprive ourselves of the need for good food, water, sunlight, or exercise. Studies have shown that loneliness can increase mortality by 50 percent—comparable to the mortality risk of smoking—and that it's about twice as dangerous as obesity.[6] It impairs immune function and boosts inflammation, which can lead to a host of diseases, such as type 2 diabetes, heart disease, and arthritis.[7] "A merry heart does good, like medicine, but a broken spirit dries the bones" (Proverbs 17:22).

John Gottman says that the difference between "masters" (couples whose relationships last) and "disasters" (couples whose relationships disintegrate) is that masters are able to repair problems.[8] Repair is the replacement for withdrawal.

Fortunately, we don't need a PhD to repair well. Apparently, the effectiveness of repair in a relationship has more to do with the recipient of the repair endeavor than the repair attempt itself. The recipient will be much more able to receive the repair attempt if the repairer has made recent deposits in his or her "emotional bank account." Talk in people's love language, be unselfish, and serve. This will make repair attempts much easier!

Denial

When we are hit with a disturbing reality, our first impulse is to deny its existence. *Denial* is a defense mechanism to keep us from having to face painful or frightening information and an unconscious refusal to accept facts. It's normal and even healthy in some situations, but as with so many adaptive aspects of human psychology, the very thing that preserves us in a crisis can destroy us if we carry it past the crisis. We need denial to a point, but we must face the truth in the long term.

What is the replacement for denial? The obvious answer is truth, but actually, truth can be discouraging. I would like to propose that we add hope and faith to the mix. Hoping your situation will improve and, indeed, exercising faith that it will, can help to create a safe environment in which to face the worst of our fears. No one can come out of the false security of denial without the true security of hope and faith.

The Bible writer Paul said, "Now abide faith, hope, love, these three; but the greatest of these is love" (1 Corinthians 13:13). Why not bring the tools of faith and hope to bear upon our relationships so that we can learn how to love and be loved?

Misinterpretation

Negatively interpreting others' motives can create terrible frustration in a relationship. We human beings love to be known and perceived correctly. In most cases, we are willing to let go of being *agreed with* if we are simply *understood.*

The replacement for misinterpreting is checking in. Don't be overconfident in your own interpretation of a matter. Check in and make sure you heard the person correctly. I use an acronym called EAR: Empathy = Ask and Reflect. The way to empathy and connection is to ask questions to draw out the other person and to reflect back what you heard this individual say in your own words.

Stuffing

Emotions start wars. Although they are invisible, weightless, and massless, they are nonetheless very real and very powerful. To attempt to avoid emotions is really to engage in a futile endeavor, for they will come out somehow.

We spend much time talking about emotion regulation, controlling our thought lives, and being rational, reasonable human beings. This is well and good. Allowing our emotions to drive our choices can harm us psychologically, relationally, and even physically—health problems and unstable emotions are connected. However, there's a tendency in human nature to go to extremes. We might reject emotionalism and end up stuffing our feelings because emotions are like children. We might not let them drive us, but we are attuned to them, listen to them, and gather valid information from them. Ultimately, we want to learn to express them.

Replace stuffing with appropriate emotional expression. One of the most important sentences you can learn is "I feel _____." Admitting the way you feel to yourself and to people you can trust can stop an emotional cascade in its tracks. Paradoxically, accepting emotion is the first step of changing it. Admitting our feelings puts us in a position where we take responsibility for what we feel. Apart from taking this responsibility, we will likely try to shift the burden to someone else, accusing and attacking him or her, thus harming the relationship.

The seven deadly relationship sins

The following table summarizes the seven deadly relationship sins and their replacements. To direct your process of change, fill out the confession inventory that follows the sin and replacement table:

Sin	Replacement
Escalation	Time-out
Invalidation	Validation
Defensiveness	Openness
Withdrawal	Repair
Denial	Hope and faith
Misinterpretation	Checking in
Stuffing	Expressing

"Therefore confess your sins to each other and pray for each other so that you may be healed. The prayer of a righteous person is powerful and effective" (James 5:16, NIV).

Confess

Rate yourself from one to ten (ten being the highest) on the deadly relationship sins.

Sin	1–10
Escalation	
Invalidation	
Defensiveness	
Withdrawal	
Denial	
Misinterpretation	
Stuffing	

Prayer

Pray the following prayer, filling in the blanks.

Dear God,

I realize I have a problem with _____. Here is how it usually occurs: _____

_____

_____

_____

_____

_____.

God, give me Your grace to change. I claim the promise, "The love of God has been poured out in our hearts by the Holy Spirit who was given to us" (Romans 5:5). Filled with Your love, I pray I will replace _____ with _____ and day by day be more completely conformed to Your image.

---

1. This tool is based on the author's web series at the Life and Health Network's website. Jennifer Jill Schwirzer, "7 Relationship Sins 00: Intro," Life and Health Network, September 16, 2015, https://lifeandhealth.org/lifestyle/7-relationship-sins-00-intro/154282.html.

2. Raymond Niaura et al., "Hostility, the Metabolic Syndrome, and Incident Coronary Heart Disease," *Health Psychology* 21, no. 6 (2002), https://psycnet.apa.org/doi/10.1037/0278-6133.21.6.588.

3. Karina W. Davidson and Elizabeth Mostofsky, "Anger Expression and Risk of Coronary Heart Disease: Evidence From the Nova Scotia Health Survey," *American Heart Journal* 159, no. 2 (February 2010), https://dx.doi.org/10.1016%2Fj.ahj.2009.11.007.

4. Scott Stanley, Daniel Trathen, Savanna McCain, and Milt Bryan, *A Lasting Promise: The Christian Guide to Fighting for Your Marriage*, rev. ed. (San Francisco, CA: Jossey-Bass, 2014), 16–33.

5. Ellie Lisitsa, "The Four Horsemen: Criticism, Contempt, Defensiveness, and Stonewalling," Gottman Institute, April 23, 2013, https://www.gottman.com/blog/the-four-horsemen-recognizing-criticism-contempt-defensiveness-and-stonewalling/.

6. Honor Whiteman, "Loneliness a Bigger Killer Than Obesity, Say Researchers," *Medical News Today*, August 6, 2017, https://www.medicalnewstoday.com/articles/318723.php.

7. Katy Hole, *Loneliness Compendium: Examples From Research and Practice* (York, UK: Joseph Rowntree Foundation, 2011), https://www.jrf.org.uk/file/41006/download?token=LZBy4VDE&filetype=full-report.

8. Kyle Benson, "Repair Is the Secret Weapon of Emotionally Connected Couples," Gottman Institute, February 23, 2017, https://www.gottman.com/blog/repair-secret-weapon-emotionally-connected-couples/.

The source of shame is the brokenness of sinful human nature. Though Adam and Eve were "not ashamed" in the beginning, the moment they fell, they "made themselves coverings" to try to compensate for their shame (Genesis 2:25; 3:7). This posed a problem, as human shame is too deep for human effort alone to access. Life experience, upbringing, religious influences, traumas, and societal factors can compound one's sense of shame, but the taproot lies very deep and requires God's healing touch. Here are some steps toward that healing:

1. *Accept feelings of shame as the consequence of sin.* Don't expect to live a shame-free life. In fact, depending upon your temperament, you may always struggle with some feelings of shame. Don't personalize those feelings; don't assume they mean more than they do. Unless you have clear evidence that you have done something wrong, don't assume you have. Don't assume you are worse than other people. In other words, observe the feelings of shame, accept them as feelings, but don't attach to them meaning that they don't have.

2. *Bring those feelings of shame to Jesus.* He "endured the cross, despising the shame" (Hebrews 12:2). He knows just how you feel. "This feeling of guiltiness must be laid at the foot of the cross of Calvary. The sense of sinfulness has poisoned the springs of life and true happiness. Now Jesus says, 'Lay it all on Me; I will take your sin, I will give you peace. Destroy no longer your self-respect, for I have bought you with the price of My own blood. You are Mine; your weakened will I will strengthen; your remorse for sin, I will remove.' "[1]

3. *Ask God to forgive any known sins, and give Him permission to show you any sins you don't know of.* "If we confess our sins, He is faithful and just to forgive us our sins and to cleanse us from all unrighteousness" (1 John 1:9). "Therefore let us, as many as are mature, have this mind; and if in anything you think otherwise, God will reveal even this to you" (Philippians 3:15). Don't rely on your feelings to tell you whether something is wrong; rely on the Word of God and the Holy Spirit, who is just, reasonable, and redemptive.

4. *Apologize and repair the damage with any others involved as much as can be done without causing further damage.* There are some situations where contacting those we have harmed will only worsen the situation. Pray for discernment, and counsel with others to make that determination.

5. *Once you have asked God to forgive you and made reparations with other people, believe in grace.* "For by grace you have been saved through faith" (Ephesians 2:8). This is where the battle over our feelings of shame tends to begin. This is where faith must lay hold of the promises of God. It will help you tremendously if you talk and act out your faith rather than expressing doubt. "Talk and act as if your faith was invincible."[2]

Creative ways to handle shame

Here are some creative ways you can live out your faith by handling shame well:

Gratitude. Try being thankful for what you have. For instance, if you have body shame, remember that you are "fearfully and wonderfully made" (Psalm 139:14). If you have ten fingers and toes, praise God for it. You may not have a full head of hair, but you have a head. Try to be grateful for what you have and care for it.

Humor. Whatever your quirks and limitations may be, play them up with humor. My paraplegic friend had a snorkeling club for wheelchair-bound people called the Moray Wheels. When I asked him once if I could help him fold his wheelchair to get into the car, he said, "Nah, I'm in a hurry."

Acceptance. Think pragmatically about your shame issues. One girl felt shame because of her acne. She would cover it with makeup, then feel ashamed for wearing makeup. I said, "You are going to have to accept something about yourself—either the acne or your desire to cover it up."

Opposition. Sometimes it helps to counter our sense of shame directly. Cognitive behaviorist Albert Ellis developed the banana exercise in which he would tie a banana on a string and lead it around the mall. My children used to dress up like pioneers with long dresses and bonnets and go to Walmart.

Community. Group support may help you overcome what you may not be able to conquer as an individual. Recovery groups, civil-rights advocates, support groups for physical conditions, and other groups work on this principle.

---

1. Ellen G. White, *This Day With God* (Washington, DC: Review and Herald®, 1979), 63.
2. Ellen G. White, *Christ's Object Lessons* (Battle Creek, MI: Review and Herald®, 1900), 147.

SOCIAL MEDIA DISORDER SCALE

During the past year, have you had any of the following experiences?[1]

- Regularly found that you can't think of anything else but the moment that you will be able to use social media again
- Regularly felt dissatisfied because you wanted to spend more time on social media
- Often felt bad when you couldn't use social media
- Tried to spend less time on social media but failed
- Regularly neglected other activities (e.g., hobbies, exercise) because you wanted to use social media
- Regularly had arguments with others because of your social media use
- Regularly lied to your parents or other people about the amount of time you spent on social media
- Often used social media to escape from negative feelings
- Had serious conflict with your family because of your social media use

If you answered yes to five or more of these items, you meet the criteria for a formal diagnosis of a disordered social media user. While there is no formal diagnosis of social media disorder in the *Diagnostic and Statistical Manual of Mental Disorders* (DSM-5),[2] this assessment is very similar to internet gaming disorder, which the DSM-5 lists as a condition for further study.

---

1. This tool is adapted from Regina van den Eijnden, Jeroen Lemmens, and Patti M. Valkenburg, "The Social Media Disorder Scale," *Computers in Human Behavior* 61 (2016), https://www.uu.nl/sites/default/files/social-media-disorder-scale-development-and-validation.pdf.

2. American Psychiatric Association, *Diagnostic and Statistical Manual of Mental Disorders*, 5th ed. (Arlington, VA: American Psychiatric Association, 2013).

Making good choices takes energy. Researchers went into a mall and asked shoppers how many shopping decisions they had made. Then they gave each person a series of math questions and told them to do as many as they wished. The shoppers who had made the greatest number of shopping decisions did the fewest math problems.[1] This phenomenon is called *decision fatigue.*

The frontal lobe of the cerebral cortex is what makes us fully human, moral, rational, creative, and spiritual creatures; however, to operate this part of the brain requires significant energy. Apparently, habit takes over when the orbitofrontal cortex—the decision-making, goal-directed center of the brain—becomes weary. It also works in reverse: the endocannabinoid receptors responsible for habit formation quiet the goal-directed tendencies of the orbitofrontal cortex, so the power of habit tends to take over our decision making. The point is that it behooves us to lighten the load on our brains by forming good habits. That way, when the brain is too weary to resist temptation and be moral, rational, and sensible, good habits take over.

People experience positive changes when they find and embrace something better than what they have. Dwelling on our bad habits will not yield change. They must be replaced. The following habits are my suggestions.

Habit 1: Rise early
What do the chief executive officers of General Motors, AOL, Xerox, GE, PepsiCo, Fiat Chrysler, Square, Apple, Starbucks, and Disney have in common? They are all early risers.[2] Getting busy in the early hours of the day may give us more productive hours because we sidestep traffic jams and long lines and always find a parking space. They also work better with the circadian clock. Early risers tend to go to bed earlier. Bright light early in the morning tends to raise serotonin levels, which turns to melatonin later in the day.

Habit 2: Spend time with God
Often, meditation is promoted as essential to mental health and has been scientifically shown to improve focus, mood, organization, and a host of other functions.[3] It may be that the very same benefits come from a time of prayer and Bible study. Three components are essential: First, gratitude for blessings bestowed. We would benefit from writing down and sharing at least three blessings a day. Second, inspirational reading to stretch the mind. Third, prayer that places in the hands of God the things beyond our control and asks from God power for the things we can change.

Habit 3: Eat breakfast
Early risers also have more time to eat breakfast. We put fuel in a car at the beginning of a journey, not at the end. The foundation of our nutritional intake for the day is set in the early part of the

T
O
O
L
B
O
X

day. Without breakfast, we will be inclined to grab sweet foods and coffee to raise our energy levels. These will set us up for a crash only a short time later as the pancreas pours out insulin in response to the rapid spike in blood sugar. Thus, a wild roller-coaster ride begins. A breakfast of whole grains, proteins, and fruits will gradually raise your blood sugar to a comfortable and sustainable level.

Habit 4: Have a regular schedule

Everything in nature—from the seasons to the turning of the earth, the daily cycle of the sun, and the life cycle of flora and fauna—has a schedule. "To everything there is a season," said the wise man (Ecclesiastes 3:1)! Regularity has obvious benefits in better digestion and sleep, but its hidden benefits are a greater ability to focus on things that matter most. When you don't have to decide every day when to eat, for instance, but rather let your schedule tell you, it frees up your mind to focus on other things. Meals, sleep and wake times, and work hours are the first and most important things to schedule. Be regular but not rigid.

Habit 5: Make a list of goals

Lists work to focus our minds on the tasks at hand. We should write out all that we would like to accomplish that day, then prioritize and schedule the items. Each time we check an item off the list, it will give us a boost of endorphins that will increase our motivation for the other things on the list. A word of caution: we will not always *feel* like following through. All mature individuals must learn how to do things they don't *want* to do in that moment. This is will training, or self-discipline. Our self-respect hangs on our ability to discipline ourselves. Lists can help tremendously with this.

Habit 6: Eat healthy food

Research shows that a simple diet of whole grains, fruits, nuts, and vegetables is the best for human beings. Yet the typical diet consists largely of animal products and refined foods. We should move away from animal and refined foods toward more unrefined plant foods. Often this is scary for us because it's unfamiliar. Great healthy-cooking classes are available at Whole Foods, some local Seventh-day Adventist churches, and even online. YouTube provides an endless stream of great cooking demonstrations. Try one healthy eating day per week, then two, and then three, until most of your intake is home-cooked, plant-based goodness.

Habit 7: Drink lots of water

Most, if not all, of us walk this earth in a state of mild dehydration. Typically, we reach for a cup of coffee or an energy drink when we feel flat. Caffeine can upset the delicate balance of neurotransmitters in the brain and make emotional regulation much harder. It will raise energy levels temporarily, but a crash soon follows. Many people drink coffee because their energy is low from dehydration, and they further dehydrate themselves with the caffeine, which is a diuretic. Try tapering off caffeine, and replacing coffee, tea, and soda with half an ounce to an ounce of water for every pound of body weight (for example, a two-hundred-pound person needs two hundred ounces of water per day). Having a big jar or pitcher on your desk is a good way to make sure you follow through.

Habit 8: Exercise

Besides toning the muscles, increasing lung capacity, cleansing the circulatory system, regulating digestion, and preventing a host of diseases—from heart disease to diabetes and beyond—exercise builds the brain. In particular, it increases synaptic plasticity, prevents neurodegeneration, and increases growth factors that support these positive benefits.[4] Walking is the best exercise because it works every muscle and system of the body. Brisk walking, alternating with running, is an excellent way to get strong cardiovascular exercise without spending money on a gym membership. Floor exercises or even activities such as housework, yard work, and gardening can build upper body and abdominal strength. One doesn't have to spend money to get exercise; don't let that become a barrier.

Habit 9: Manage your thought life

Our thoughts and emotions can form a feedback loop that can cycle wildly in the wrong direction. Many people don't realize that we can actually control our thought life to redirect our emotions. This is called *emotional regulation.* Often, we assume that our emotions come directly out of life experiences and circumstances, such as school pressure, uncertainty about the future, or relationship problems. In reality, the way we *feel* about things is determined by the way we *think* about them. Learning to control our thought life can be the beginning of a calmer, healthier emotional space for many people. Realize that our thoughts are like muscles—they must be worked to get stronger. If you find your thoughts are hard to control at first, keep trying; in time you will have success.

Habit 10: Manage your money

Many people go through highly specialized training and secure high-paying jobs only to fail financially because of poor money management. Every young person needs to learn the basic skills of managing a checking account, budgeting, and reading credit-card statements. But most importantly, they must learn to discriminate between wants and needs. There are many free resources (Cashcourse.org; Balancetrack.org) and some good paid courses (Dave Ramsey's Financial Peace University and Suze Orman's courses at Suzeorman.com). Simply type "free personal finance courses" into an internet search engine, and you will find a slew of options.

Habit 11: Manage your time

In a sense, time is money. It's a gift we can either manage or squander. Whatever techniques one uses for time management, the basic practice of keeping a planner is essential. Google Calendar, which is free, works well and is user-friendly. It can be synced with smartphones and computers to send alerts. Even if you have no specific appointments, you can still plan your day, allotting time for all the items on your to-do list. Be specific but not rigid. There is no need to go overboard—allow for some spontaneity. Frame out a basic schedule so that you are not floating along like a ship adrift at sea. Some people benefit from scheduling social media and email time to avoid overdoing it. If you tend to get lost in the black hole of social media, you may want to incorporate that habit.

Habit 12: Connect with others

Authentic social connection gives context and meaning to our lives. The reality is that none of us operates in a vacuum. We are all part of the great web of humanity, and we deeply, intimately, and powerfully affect one another. The competitive model of human existence leaves people lonely and unfulfilled. The cooperative model means that each success ministers to the common good. Share your journey, your goals, and your struggles with other people and ask them to support and pray for you. Then offer to do the same for them.

The will to do

Lists can be discouraging as they stare at us, reminding us of our deficiencies; however, the human will is a marvelous thing. Many cry, "I am just not motivated!" But what they really mean is that they don't *feel* like doing, or not doing, something. Motivation is bigger than feeling. It is the mysterious ability that we have to choose specific actions in spite of our feelings, appetites, and drives.

However, the will can become paralyzed, particularly in the face of long-established habits or addictions. This is where God's power comes into the process. The first and second steps of the twelve-step process of Alcoholics Anonymous are as follows:

1. We admitted we were powerless over alcohol—that our lives had become unmanageable.
2. We came to believe that a Power greater than ourselves could restore us to sanity.

Recognizing our powerlessness to change is actually the first step toward change. The second is to look up to heaven and receive power from outside of ourselves. Then when the human and divine wills intertwine, their combined synergy gives birth to change.

As mentioned, human support is part of the health equation. Other people can't give us divine power, but they can encourage us to receive it, and they can give accountability and structure to the change process.

In the words of researcher Charles Duhigg, "Habits are malleable throughout your entire life."[5] It's never too late to form better ones.

---

1. John Tierney, "Do You Suffer From Decision Fatigue?" *New York Times*, August 17, 2011, https://www.nytimes.com/2011/08/21/magazine/do-you-suffer-from-decision-fatigue.html.

2. Denis Lesak, "24 Successful People Who Wake Up Really (Really) Early," *Medium*, November 7, 2015, https://medium.com/@denislesak/24-successful-people-who-wake-up-really-really-early-da1b05559c58.

3. Erin Brodwin, "9 Surprising Ways Meditation Changes Your Brain," *Business Insider*, April 17, 2017, https://www.businessinsider.com/meditation-effects-benefits-science-2017-3.

4. Seung-Soo Baek, "Role of Exercise on the Brain," *Journal of Exercise Rehabilitation* 12, no. 5 (2016): 380–385, https://dx.doi.org/10.12965%2Fjer.1632808.404.

5. Charles Duhigg, "Habits: How They Form and How to Break Them," interview by Terry Gross, *Fresh Air*, March 5, 2012, https://www.npr.org/2012/03/05/147192599/habits-how-they-form-and-how-to-break-them.

NOTES